Caroline Ellis:
Homemaker of the Airwaves

By Ryan Ellett

Caroline Ellis: Homemaker of the Airwaves
By Ryan Ellett
Copyright © 2020 Ryan Ellett
No part of this book may be reproduced in any form or by any means, electronic, mechanical, digital, photocopying, or recording, except for inclusion of a review, without permission in writing from the publisher or Author.

No copyright is claimed for the photos within this book. They are used for the purposes of publicity only.

Published in the USA by:
BearManor Media
4700 Millenia Blvd.
Suite 175 PMB 90497
Orlando, FL 32839
www.bearmanormedia.com

Paperback ISBN: 978-1-62933-582-7
Case ISBN: 978-1-62933-583-4
BearManor Media, Orlando, Florida
Printed in the United States of America
Book design by Robbie Adkins, www.adkinsconsult.com
Cover background image Adobe Stock.

Ryan Ellett

*For Jim Beshires.
A dear friend. No one was more dedicated to the preservation
of old-time radio.*

Table of Contents

Acknowledgements vii

Introduction: Women in Early Radio ix

Part 1: The Early Life of Caroline Crockett Ellis 1

Part 2: Ellis Arrives on Radio. 12

Part 3: Big Time: *Caroline's Golden Store* 45

Part 4: Back in Kansas City 76

Appendix: *Happy Home* Script Selections and Summaries . . . 103

Index 127

Acknowledgements

This book would not have happened were it not for a short email I received out of the blue from a complete stranger in January 2016. In it, Steve Crockett shared how pleased he was to read an old piece I'd written about his great-Aunt, Caroline Ellis, a pioneering radio personality. This was pleasant in and of itself as historians – especially in this field – rarely get feedback about their work. Mr. Crockett was referring to an article I had published about Ellis in *Radiogram*, a magazine published by the old-time radio hobby organization SPERDVAC (Society to Preserve and Encourage Radio Drama, Variety and Comedy) in 2012. The piece was based on research I had done two years before that and presented at Kansas State University's 5th Annual Great Plains Radio History Symposium in 2010. The article had eventually been placed online by SPERDVAC and members of Ellis' family had discovered it by accident. I wound up most of the research about Ellis five years earlier so by the time of Mr. Crockett's email I had moved on to other research areas, having reported out as much as could be gleaned from the resources available at the time.

One comment in the email, however, grabbed my attention. Mr. Crockett mentioned off-handedly that "[he still had] some of her scripts and writings." Original radio documentation from this era, especially in private hands unencumbered by the restrictions that can come with using library and archival sources, can be a rare find. An exchange of emails led to a short 30-minute drive down the interstate to meet with Steve at his home in Topeka, KS. The mementos of Caroline's career that he mentioned in his email turned out to include not only broadcast scripts but invaluable family histories, numerous high-quality photographs of Caroline's radio years, and unpublished stories and poems. Six years after I first shed some feeble rays of light on an overlooked twenty-year radio career in one article and presentation, I suddenly had access to a wealth of primary documents that offered the opportunity to present a far more well-rounded and in-depth study of her entire life.

But what to do with these new resources? I considered an updated article but too much material would have to be left out and it would only be seen by a tiny potential readership. I wanted to be able to share and explore the entirety of Ellis' work and felt her story was worthy of a wider audience. Almost upon seeing the family trove of historical treasures a little voice began to insist that Ellis' life deserved to be told in a book of her own. Still, writing a book of any kind is no small undertaking and it took another two years of fits and starts and hammering away at an outline to figure out how to present this amazing life within the context of the eras in which she lived. Nevertheless, with the encouragement of Ellis' family and others in the old-time radio community, after almost a decade of attention her story prevailed and can now be read and appreciated in full.

No one was more encouraging of this writing than the late Jim Beshires, founder of the Old Time Radio Researchers group. He always had a hopeful word when it seemed like the project was going nowhere. Don Frey, a fifty-year veteran of the old-time radio hobby, was my most enthusiastic backer. He heard my original presentation way back in 2010 and accompanied me on my initial visit to obtain Ellis' personal papers. Martin Grams was the first to insist that these documents must be turned into a full book. There are far too many people who have answered questions big and small along the way but the vast majority of them belong to the wonderful preservation organizations SPERDVAC and Old-Time Radio Researchers.

Introduction

The first two decades of broadcasting over the airwaves from the late 1890s to the years just preceding World War I consisted of streams of "dits" and "dahs," the two unique audio bursts used in Samuel Morse's code. Initially developed for telegraph lines that began to crisscross the United States as railroads stretched westward during the mid-1800s, the communication code was adapted by users of the formerly wired telegraphy that was now giving way to wireless telegraphy, eventually known as radio. Until World War I traffic on the airwaves was found primarily in the heavy industrial fields of shipping and transportation, especially seaborne vessels, and to a lesser extent, a small number of amateur hobbyists or "hams."

These professionals and hobbyists sent messages across the country and around the world, pounding out Morse code on home-built transmitters. Users often developed their own unique "voice" in this so-far voiceless medium, unique rhythms and cadences in sending code. Referred to as one's "fist" (reflecting the skilled hand tapping on a telegraph key), radio operators could identify other operators by their Morse code transmissions.

Because voice transmission was rare and still somewhat experimental into the 19-teens, an operator's sex was ostensibly hidden from others with no voice to use as an identifying marker. Yet the field – both among professionals and amateurs – was primarily one of males. In painting a picture of early 20th century radio amateurs, broadcasting historian Michelle Hilmes notes that, similar to late 20th century computer geek culture, the developing technology was seen as the province of young middle-class white males. Further preventing women from participating in wireless was the need to build one's own radio, usually from published schematics. The requisite higher mathematical skills in addition to manual knowledge such as carpentry, soldering, and mechanical construction were subjects reluctantly taught to most women. Not until the 1920s could enthusiasts visit a neighborhood store and walk home with a fully functional radio unit. Nevertheless, women (and non-whites) staked out a place in the field even if they were ignored by other operators and the press that covered them.

While women everywhere struggled to earn employment outside the home, a small handful managed to gain employment as ship-to-shore telegraphers as early as 1910 (including Gladys Kathleen Parkin and Graynella Packer) and qualified to be licensed by the federal government just two years later with the Radio Act of 1912. Just as often, however, they were denied such work even when earned against their male peers. As the military began to recognize the value of radio communication during World War I, by 1918 the Navy was explicitly banning women from enlisting as radio operators. While several had been allowed to enlist at the war's outbreak, the Navy ultimately determined that their employment was "impracticable." Eventually authorities encouraged interested women operators to apply for civilian wireless jobs, thus allowing male operators to enlist for Naval duty. It was reported in early 1919 that Reavis Hughes had satisfactorily completed an operator's course at Los Angeles' Polytechnic High School and subsequently passed the all-day exam to earn her first-grade operator license. Her application was ultimately denied when officials in Washington, D.C. learned she was female. British shippers avoided hiring any women operators to work onboard on the premise that they were unable to climb up masts when needed to make repairs. They were, however, open to hiring them as shorebound operators. Even when they did manage to gain entry to the wireless field, females were still seen as an "other," receiving the official Morse code designation YL (Young Lady) in 1920 to distinguish them from male operators who referred to each as OM (Old Man).

A small handful of women managed to make inroads with stations in non-broadcasting roles. Thanks to the work of the preeminent historian of female broadcasters, Donna Halper, Eunice Randall has earned a belated bit of recognition. Hired by the American Radio and Research Company (AMRAD) of Massachusetts in 1918, she first worked on drawing technical plans then actually tested these primitive radio products. In a field assumed to be the domain of men, Randall even promoted this equipment to the public. Although it soon became common to find women in many secretarial duties around radio station offices, examples can be found of women who earned more esteemed roles such as program directors. Eleanor Nesbitt Poehler was hired in this capacity for Minneapolis' WLAG because of her musical contacts, a necessity in the early 1920s when live entertainment was the norm and needed to be procured sometimes on short notice. Ada Morgan O'Brien of San Francisco had the same responsibility for some Bay Area stations. Jessie E. Koewing pulled double-duty for WOR in Newark where she was not only on the air as an announcer but the station manager behind the scenes as well. Halper has even pinpointed the first woman known to have owned a radio station (built by her husband), Marie Zimmerman of WIAE in Vinton, IA, in 1922. Randall, Poehler, and Zimmerman represented outliers in the radio industry, however, with their behind-the-scenes responsibilities. The following excerpt from a 1921 *Wireless Age*, though intended in a humorous vein, seems to accurately represent the general attitude of radio men toward their female colleagues:

> The Radio Woman
> When she talks too long (Interrupter). If she argues incorrectly (Converter). If she is willing to come your way (Meter). If she wants to see your set (Conductor.) If she wants to be a nangel (Transformer). When she is sulky (Exciter). If she gets too excited (Controller). If she proves your circuit is wrong (Compensator). If she is wrong (Rectifier). If she goes up in the air (Condenser). If she wants chocolates (Feeder). If she sings false (Tuner). If she is a poor companion (Discharger). If she gossips too much (Regulator). If she fumes and sputters (Insulator). If she fancies someone else (Reverser).

Most women involved in broadcasting during this era had, instead, primarily on-air performing responsibilities.

As post-World War I commercial radio began to develop a business model dependent upon paid advertising, women earned a place behind the microphone as singers, actresses, and commentators. Unfortunately for the growing number of women whose imaginations were sparked by the idea of performing over the airwaves, the primitive microphones of the early 1920s did a poor job of conveying higher-pitched voices. Whether it was purely a technical issue or because predominantly male engineering teams designed the mics to work best with voice qualities similar to their own, station managers were extremely touchy about how females sounded on the air. Those who had mid-range and lower voices or who could affect those tones as needed earned more sustaining success.

The airwaves of the early 1920s were filled with music, informational or educational talks, and narrated sports broadcasts, and women found numerous opportunities in the first two areas. Classical and lite-classical music possibly filled more airtime during the first decade of commercial radio than any other single musical style, especially on the larger metropolitan stations, but just about every genre of music in fashion at the time received some airtime and women could regularly be heard on many of them. Opera vocalists were most often heard solo, and magazines such as *Wireless Age* regularly featured profiles of stage stars who were discovering the power of radio to spread their name to new potential fans. Occasionally heard solo, women more often were placed with a male group of musicians, serving two purposes for the act aside from the straight musical talent they could offer. First, a woman fronting a band brought an automatic level of respectability, softening any roughneck image of the remaining male musicians. Second, and perhaps most important, a female face made for better promotional posters. While looks didn't matter on the radio, many if not most musical air acts were expected and even required to participate in live performances around a listening region and an attractive face came in useful trying to sell additional tickets.

At the same time a very few women were earning paychecks as broadcast engineers and program directors and more were entertaining audiences with their music, others were beginning to carve out their own space on the airwaves that would become uniquely theirs for the span of radio's Golden Age and beyond. These spaces were dedicated to areas traditionally considered the feminine domain, including meal preparation, household care, child rearing, and managing the family budget. It is impossible to identify the first homemaker of the air as the programming would broadly become known, but by the mid-1920s nearly every station, large and small and in towns and cities of every size, had some such programming.

The metropolitan stations have left a better historical record both because they tended to be more powerful, thus reaching a wider audience, and because the larger city newspapers were more likely to cover early broadcasting events. KDKA (Pittsburgh), for instance, dedicated evening air time in 1922 to programs such as *Garden & Home Beautifying*, *Weekly Fashion Letter of Interest to Women*, and *Home Furnishing – Modern and Practical*. Chicago's KYW in December 1922 introduced *The Housewife's Hour* featuring Anna J. Peterson, director of the home service department of the Peoples Gas Light and Coke Company. Described as an authority on cooking domestic science, Peterson focused her talks on recipes and related meal information. Des Moines' WHO was already featuring feminine programming during morning slots, times when homemaking broadcasts would regularly be featured for decades to come. As early as 1922 the station aired "special items of interest to women" on Mondays, Wednesdays, and Saturdays.

On the West Coast by 1926 KFI in Los Angeles was airing *Betty Crocker Gold Medal Flour Home Service Talk* weekdays at 10:45 while Portland's KGW aired a hefty program from 9:45 to 11:30 a.m. featuring "Women's Daily Dozen," household helps, and a "shopping guide" to listeners. Prudence Penny advised homemakers in Seattle from 11:30 to noon on her program *What to Prepare for Tonight's Dinner*. One of the few books devoted to the history of a single radio station is Robert Birkby's 1985 history of KMA, a rural station in Shenandoah, IA, 60 miles southeast of Omaha. His work not only confirms the presence of such female-oriented programming as home gardening, flower arranging, and domestic science talks on mid-1920s rural stations, it suggests that women presenters and performers made up an even greater percentage of on-air talent than in more urban outlets.

One sample radio schedule from a Wednesday in 1926 demonstrates the extent to which women's programming centered on homemaking-related activities was the norm across the radio dial schedule. Because so many of these stations served listening audiences far beyond their originating cities, times were given in all four continental time zones (Eastern Standard Time listed).

Tonight's Dinner (WWJ, Detroit, 9:30 a.m.)
Menu (WIP, Philadelphia, 10:00 a.m.)
Women's Hour (WJZ, New York, 10:00 a.m.)
Home Service Talk with Betty Crocker (WEAF, New York, and WFI, Philadelphia, 10:45 a.m.)
Talk to Housewives with Mrs. Lydia Flanders (WTAG, Worcester, MA, 10:45 a.m.)
Women's Club with Jean Sargent (WHT, Shenandoah, IA, 11:00 a.m.)
Women's Program (WNYC, New York, 11:00 a.m.)
Food Fads and Fancies with Betty Crocker (WCCO, Minneapolis, 11:45 a.m.)
Home Service Talk with Betty Crocker (WDAF, Kansas City, WJAR, Providence, RI, WHT, Shenandoah, IA, 11:45 a.m.)
Household Hints (WGN, Chicago, noon)
Home Economics (WQJ, Chicago, noon)
Fashion and Household Talks (WEBH, Chicago, 12:30 p.m.)
Discussion of Fashions (WGN, Chicago, 12:30 p.m.)
Table Talk (KYW, Chicago, 12:35 p.m.)
Sewing Talk (KPO, San Francisco, 1:00 p.m.)
Woman's Hour (WCCO, Minneapolis, 3:00 p.m.)
Cooking School (WLW, Cincinnati, 4:00 p.m.)
Home Management with Aunt Jane (WOC, Davenport, IA, 4:00 p.m.)
Health Assurance with Jean Rich (WQJ, Chicago, 4:00 p.m.)
Housekeeper's Half Hour (KOAC, Corvallis, OR, 5:00 p.m.)
Recipes (WMAQ, Chicago, 5:00 p.m.)
Hints for Housekeeper (KGO, San Francisco, 6:00 p.m.)
Today's Recipes (KFOA, Seattle, 7:00 p.m.)
Woman's Hour (KLX, Oakland, 7:00 p.m.)
Domestic Science Talk (KMA, Shenandoah, IA, 7:00 p.m.)
Talk with Sara Prentiss (KOAC, Corvallis, OR, 10:30 p.m.)
Talk with Emma Weld (KOAC, Corvallis, OR, 10:45 p.m.)

In addition to firmly cementing their place on broadcast schedules with a wide variety of programs aimed at mothers and wives maintaining their households, women also managed to get a toehold in the related genre of soap operas that began to gain wide audiences in the late 1920s and early 1930s. Arising out of daily dramatic evening serials including *Sam 'n' Henry*, *The Smith Family*, and *The Rise of the Goldbergs*, foremost soaps historian Jim Cox confirms the long-established claim that *Painted Dreams*, created and written by a woman, Irna Phillips, deserves recognition as initiating the soap opera era.

Outside the homemaker broadcasts, women possibly found no stronger footing in the radio industry than in the production of soap operas. With few exceptions, in fact, the names most associated with so-called washboard weepers were women. Anne Hummert stood as one of – if not the most – powerful figures in radio soap opera along with husband Frank. Together they created and oversaw dozens of serials while delegating the actual writing to a stable of authors. Their programs filled more than four hours of weekly air time at one point (in 15-minute installments) and Cox estimates they alone were responsible for more than half of daytime radio's income. Hummert's power and influence within the industry was such that she shrugged off network and sponsor pressure to avoid certain actors and writers who over the years were tarnished by left-wing associations.

The aforementioned Phillips arguably sits next to or only slightly below Anne Hummert atop the sudsy genre, having on her own created not only the original soap *Painted Dreams*, but the longest lived serial of all time, *The Guiding Light*. Debuting in 1937, that series ran on radio until 1956 and then television until 2009, a 72-year-long story. Her *Road of Life* and *Right to Happiness* both aired 21 years apiece while *Today's Children*, *The Brighter Day*, and *Joyce Jordan, M.D.* each ran for years. In the 1940s she was placing an entire one-hour broadcast block with General Mills.

Elaine Carrington held her own with Hummert's and Phillips' impressive productions, creating and writing *Pepper Young's Family* (and its predecessors), *When A Girl Marries*, and *Rosemary* from the 1930s into the 1950s. Unlike her peers, Carrington authored her own scripts, her output topping 40,000 words per week at the peak of her programs' popularity.

It was in these two broadcasting genres that Caroline Ellis would carve out her own twenty-year radio career. She arrived in the industry too late to be considered a trailblazer in either homemaking or serial radio, but she made unique contributions to both that only now have been uncovered to be shared with the wider world.

Part 1: The Early Life of Caroline Crockett Ellis

The Crockett Family

The family of Caroline Crockett Ellis proudly boasts that she could claim descent from none other than David Stern Crockett, the legendary frontiersman who served the state of Tennessee in the United States House of Representatives from 1827 - 1831 and again from 1833 - 1835 and lost his life at the Battle of the Alamo on March 6, 1836. Though the claim that she was a great-niece to Crockett is hazy and difficult to prove conclusively through genealogical listings, her ancestral line is additionally distinguished through the service of her great grandfather, Asher Crockett (1760 - 1846), a native-born Virginian who ran away from home at the age of 16 to serve in George Washington's army. Originally a waiter, Crockett was officially recognized as an enlisted soldier (under the name James Anderson) between 1778 and 1783 during which time he fought in the Battles of Camden, Cowpens, Guilford Court House, Hanging Rock, and Yorktown.

Asher married Sarah Blankenship on September 11, 1800, in Christiansburg, VA, and it was one of their sons, Peter Marshall Crockett, who eventually moved a branch of the Crockett family to the Midwest. Peter (1804 - 1863) felt the call of the ministry and became an ordained Methodist minister. After marrying Nancy Spurlock they welcomed a son, Stephen Marshall Crockett, into their home in Cabell, VA (now WV) on January 8, 1836. A dozen years later in 1848 Peter was summoned to Shawnee Mission, KS, to teach agricultural skills to Native Americans. There he worked on the Shawnee Indian Mission founded by the Rev. Thomas Johnson, namesake of Johnson County, the suburban Kansas City county that is the most populous in the state of Kansas. Crockett taught agricultural skills for six years to the Shawnee and other Native children who were housed at the Mission. In 1854 with the passage of the Kansas - Nebraska Act Peter moved his family again, this time to a claim west of Lawrence, KS, in Douglas County, the next county to the west of Johnson County. Two years later they relocated yet again, this time within Douglas county but just outside Lecompton to the northwest of Lawrence. Next year in 1857 a Constitutional Convention was convened in Lecompton where the members drew up the first constitution for the Territory of Kansas that would have admitted it as a slave-holding state.

Northeastern Kansas was ripped apart by the Civil War and the Crockett family reflected those raw wounds that were slow to heal, if they ever did at all. Stephen joined the Union Army as a wagon master while his two brothers shared Confederate sympathies. One brother, Jack, rose to be a captain in the Confederate army while the other brother, Jacob, remained a slaveholder in Kansas City as long as he could. The rift between the brothers was irreparable and Stephen's grandchildren don't recall him ever speaking of either Jack or Jacob, nor were the Confederate apologists really even known to the family.

Stephen Crockett married Matilda "Tillie" P. Hurst and the marriage led to four children. The first, Louis Albert, was born in 1870 and died before his first birthday. The eldest surviving son, Robert Marshall, was born next in 1875 and died in 1946. Caroline Hurst Crockett was born July 10, 1877 (and would outlive all her siblings), and her sister, Minnie Gertrude Crockett, the youngest child of Stephen and Matilda, was born in 1882. Caroline was named after her aunt Caroline Matilda Crockett, her father's older sister.

A tall man for the time, at least six feet, Caroline's father Stephen Crockett is remembered as being proud and sober with a dry sense of humor; a smile did not come easily to his face. He loved, however, to tell jokes and regale listeners with stories that often stretched the limits of believability. This love was passed down to his daughter Caroline who would come to love entertaining her listening audience, though Stephen would not live long enough to hear his daughter's radio work. He ran a general store successfully enough to raise his family of five, selling it in old age when he and wife Matilda moved in with Caroline.

Young Adult

Caroline's first job was teaching at Matney School about a mile north of Richland, KS, a few miles west of Lawrence. Nothing is known of Ellis' teaching career, a common one for young women at the time though her five-foot-ten-inch frame was unusually imposing among women and may have assisted her in establishing discipline at the country school. Very likely she resigned her spot – and the mile walk each day to and from the schoolhouse – when she married Charles Edgar Ellis, a man who was able to sustain the couple on his income after they moved to Holliday, a tiny town in Johnson County.

Caroline Ellis, ca. 1900. Courtesy Steve Crockett.

There Charles got a job as a railway mail clerk earning $200 per month, much to the chagrin of his father-in-law, Stephen Crockett, who felt that was a ridiculous salary for such a cushy job. Despite his comfortable pay from the railroad, Charles was always looking for opportunities to add to his income. At different points he raised hogs, bought and resold baled straw, and during World War I sold horses to the United States Army. The couple's financial anxieties were lessened when they learned early in their marriage that children were not going to be in their future. Instead, Charles and

Caroline Ellis, ca. 1910. Courtesy Steve Crockett.

Caroline would dote on their nephews. The couple traded the relatively rich soil found around Richland for 30-40 acres of what they discovered to be generally hard red clay in Holliday. Luckily the soil quality was of little consequence for the Crockett's; they did not count on its fertility for any household income. Two-thirds of the acreage was timber and except for a small parcel set aside for a small house and garden, the rest was in hay.

Eventually, the Ellis' modest living space was upgraded to a much larger home built entirely of stone and concrete with full electric and plumbing, luxuries in rural Kansas in the 19-teens. The new place included a full basement, a library, and a grand piano on the main floor. Family historian Beam Crockett recalled in 1975 that the house was the finest in which he ever stayed.

After the couple was comfortably established in Holliday, Caroline began to indulge two of her interests that would bring her much joy until the end of her life: writing and entertaining. She was a woman who loved new ideas and couldn't get enough of new experiences. Even in her younger years Caroline hosted associates whom her nephew described as sharing her "literary mind." Her great-nephew, Steve Crockett, concurred with that assessment and in recalling his years as a boy living with "Aunt Carrie," commented frequently on the wide assortment of guests that she enjoyed having visit and even stay for a time at her home. This did not always sit well with her family, especially her father Stephen Crockett who was very disapproving of an Indian acquaintance who visited the farm many times one summer.

Ellis also began writing in earnest, even penning a regular column – under her own name, no less – in the now-defunct *Kansas City Post*. A seemingly far-fetched opportunity for a woman with little to no formal writing training and little publishing experience, the writing assignment with the *Post* came about through her friendship with a Dr. Burris Atkins Jenkins, a man who would be instrumental in her entry to radio many years later.

Dr. Burris A. Jenkins

Jenkins was a Kansas City clergyman, the pastor of Linwood Boulevard Christian Church. Born in Kansas City in 1869, Jenkins spent the first part of his life in academia after attending college at Bethany College in West Virginia where he earned a Bachelor of Arts in 1891, then Harvard where he completed degrees in 1895 and 1896, and finally Kentucky Wesleyan College where he achieved his Doctor of Divinity in 1903. While pastoring in Indianapolis from 1896 to 1900 he was a Professor of New Testament Literature and Exegesis at the University of Indianapolis (a Methodist-affiliated school) and then briefly the head of Butler College's (now University) religion department from 1899 to 1900. Between 1901 and 1906 Jenkins served as the president of Kentucky's Transylvania University, during which time it absorbed the women's Hamilton College that then operated as a two-year institution.

Upon returning to Kansas City Jenkins resumed pastoring full time but devoted much of his free time to social causes and writing. He accepted the job of editor at the *Kansas City Post* and in that position from 1919 - 1921 advocated fiercely for the League of Nations. In the long run, however, Jenkins couldn't lead both a paper and a church and chose to step down from the former and devote his full energy to his divine calling. During these post-World War years he made the acquaintance of Caroline Ellis while participating in the Quill Club of Kansas City, a local literary society. He hired Ellis to pen regular columns for the *Post*, some of which

Dr. Burris Jenkins. From author's collection.

also appeared in the *Denver Post* due to the overlap in ownership of the two newspapers.

Hard Times

Caroline's parents moved in with her and Charles in the 19-teens and her mother Matilda passed away in 1918. The cause is unknown but this is the period during which the Spanish Flu swept around the world leading to the deaths of tens of millions. Caroline's father Stephen was a broken man afterward, managing to find some comfort only in his daily tasks of tending the garden and raising a few cattle and hogs on the hardscrabble land. Two years after Matilda's death Stephen met his own end when he was hit by a train. The Santa Fe railroad tracks cut through a part of the Crockett land Stephen daily had to cross while leading the cows to water at Mill Creek. As he must have known the daily train schedules, the family later mused on whether this had truly been an accident; one grandson recalled that he didn't "think [grandad] was ever happy after grandma died."

Losing both parents in a two-year span was difficult for Caroline but a full tragedy struck three years later when her husband Charles died suddenly in 1923. Economic times had been good for the Ellis family. With partner Ed Patterson, Charles had just purchased a forty-acre plot of prime farmland near Olathe, KS, and its investment potential seemed very promising. Not long after closing the land purchase, however, Charles came down with what the doctors diagnosed as yellow jaundice. Though uncommon in adults it is not unheard of and Charles' case proved fatal. After a month of illness, he was taken to the Eleanor Taylor Bell Memorial Hospital in Kansas City, KS (which later was subsumed into the University of Kansas Medical Center) and to the surprise of his family passed away quickly.

Crushed by the loss of her husband, Caroline was not initially worried about finances despite neither coming from a family of means nor having a job herself. It was not long before she discovered, to her dismay, that in purchasing the forty acres in Olathe with partner Ed Patterson, Charles had borrowed his portion of the down payment from Patterson. With some loan payments on the land coming due and no cash to fulfill her portion, Caroline was forced to transfer the entire title over to Patterson, leaving her with no part in the investment.

Now, for the first time in over two decades, Ellis found herself having to go back to work. She rented out the couple's house in Holliday and moved to Kansas City where, with no real training to get the attention of employers, she took a job as a housekeeper at the Densmore Hotel. The pay was modest but it came with a room at the hotel that helped compensate for the low income.

Caroline Ellis, ca. 1920. Courtesy Steve Crockett.

Ellis' writing and her friendship with Dr. Burris Jenkins – even after both severed their connections with the *Post* – helped carry her through this difficult time. The author of numerous religious-themed fiction novels during his lifetime, Burris' *The Bracegirdle* was reviewed by Ellis in a 1922 issue of the *Midwest Bookman*.

The Densmore Hotel ca. 1919. From author's collection.

The same year her husband died, 1923, Ellis participated in the 18th annual meeting of the Kansas Authors Club. Held in Topeka, it was touted as the largest such gathering in the group's history and it was presided over by J. W. Searson, professor of English at the University of Nebraska. Among the topics covered at the conference were "Improving Kansas Standards," "Short Stories and Poems," and the one which Ellis led along with Marco Morrow of Topeka and O. D. Burton of Kansas City, "The Publisher's Side of It." At the club's May meeting in Wichita she talked about "The Mission of the Book."

Ellis' writing activities did little to supplement her hotel wages, unfortunately, and after two years at the Densmore Caroline's sister Gertrude, or Gertie to much of the family, invited Caroline to come live with her in Detroit. With no bright job prospects in Kansas City, Caroline took up her sister's offer and for the first time in her life left the northeast Kansas and Kansas City region. Interestingly, while Caroline was widely recognized in her later years to be broad-minded and cosmopolitan, it was her younger sister Gertie who had lived a more worldly life up to that point.

Gertrude Crockett and Detroit

Born five years after Caroline, Gertrude left home as soon as she could to move to Kansas City where she married a man named Harlan Wells. He died a few years after their wedding and Gertrude continued to live on her own in the city until meeting and marrying Nebraska-native George Mosshart, a reporter for the *Kansas City Star*. Soon after their wedding in 1911 the newlyweds moved to Washington, D.C. where he reported on national affairs. There Gertrude's only son, Crockett Mosshart, was born in 1914. Still living in tiny Holliday, KS, Caroline must have read with a twinge of jealousy about her sister's work as president of the Woman's Suffrage Council in Washington as well as the postcards that began arriving from Europe. Gertrude took a job as an administrator in Herbert Hoover's U.S. Food Administration upon the country's entry into World War I and subsequently toured the continent as part of her work.

At the too-young age of 33 Gertrude's husband George Mosshart died on October 12, 1918, just a few months after being drafted into the war and leaving Gertrude a widow for the second time, now with a four-year-old child. She married a third time and moved to Detroit; details of the marriage, including the husband's name, remain a mystery, but her line of the Crockett family can be found in Michigan to this day.

Joining Gertrude in Detroit shortly before the Christmas of 1923, Caroline found a city that was not only three times the size of Kansas City but growing just as fast, gaining half a million new residents in the previous decade and on pace to add another half million during the 1920s. Powered by the exploding automobile industry, office buildings, hotels, and department stores were sprouting everywhere one looked in this so-called "Paris of the West." Ellis quickly found work in the J. L. Hudson Store, the flagship building of the J. L. Hudson department store chain located downtown on Woodward Avenue. After the holiday season Ellis was transferred to the ready-to-wear department. There, in what would become the second-largest department store in the world by World War II, she worked her way up to the position of purchaser of women's clothing for the entire store within a year. Exhilarated by her newfound success, in the early summer of 1924 Ellis took a position with Crowley, Milner and Company – commonly called Crowley's – another Detroit department store that competed fiercely with Hudson's. Finally experiencing a string of good fortune after a rough patch of years losing her husband and parents, a last bit of bad news came a year later in 1925. Back in Holliday, KS the family home caught fire and burned completely to the ground. While the renters were safe the structure was a complete loss. She carried no insurance on the property so that little extra income from her married years was now gone.

Caroline worked hard learning the ins and outs of the retail industry and was promoted to manager of the company's superintendent's office by 1928. After five years in Detroit Ellis' life had reached a new point of quiet and stability. In an era when the average woman's life expectancy was just over 60 years and she had just passed 50, Ellis was beginning to successfully reinvent herself. For most of her adult years up until this point she had been a worldly-oriented stay-at-home wife who dabbled in writing. Forced to move on, Ellis was able to earn a level of financial independence and professional identification that many women of the time could not earn for themselves. However, for reasons unknown, she chose not to remain in Detroit but return to Kansas City.

Part 2: Ellis Arrives on Radio

KMBC

Now one of Kansas City's major media outlets, in 1932 KMBC was owned by the Midland Broadcasting Company (hence the MBC in KMBC) whose president, Arthur B. Church, had an extensive background in radio. He began operating commercial-grade transmitters under amateur and non-profit call signs as early as 1921 but by 1928 recognized he had to get serious with broadcasting. Competition, especially from the *Kansas City Star*-owned and NBC-affiliated WDAF, was increasing dramatically and Church needed a way to become more viable in the booming industry. The answer was to join the upstart Columbia Broadcasting System (CBS) that had been founded just a year earlier under William S. Paley's strong hand. As the network's western-most station at the time, KMBC would have access to more broadcast content and programming

Arthur B. Church. From author's collection.

with a higher level of talent than Church could reasonably expect to find in Kansas City and afford to produce on his own.

Arthur Church, a devoted member of the Reorganized Church of Jesus Christ of Latter Day Saints (since renamed Community of Christ), may have been at a financial disadvantage even in partnership with CBS, but his keen eye for talent ensured KMBC was attracting some of the area's best performers. The list of entertainers who began long and illustrious broadcasting careers on KMBC between 1928 and 1933 is very impressive considering the size of the station and its market.

No KMBC alum is more famous in radio history than Goodman Ace, writer and actor on the sophisticated nationwide comedy *Easy Aces* who in years later became the most highly paid writer in television penning for the likes of Perry Como and Milton Berle. Only slightly less remembered is Hugh Studebaker who climbed his way to the top echelon of daytime serials after moving to Chicago in 1933 and had a career that lasted the length of radio's Golden Age; his name is still widely recognized by aficionados today.

While not in the top tier of performers like Ace and Studebaker, few broadcasters could boast of a career to match Ted Malone. Known by his birthname, Frank Alden Russell, when he started spending time at Arthur Church's broadcast studios while still in high school, Malone entered the profession directly upon graduation in the mid-1920s and cut his teeth for a decade at KMBC. Malone eventually succumbed to the wider broadcasting opportunities in New York and from there he hosted a number of coast-to-coast radio series during radio's Golden Age. Malone's following was so devoted that he managed to stay on the airwaves for sixty years until 1987.

Even the mid-level performers Church nurtured at his station were good enough to earn sponsored network shows at times. The Texas Rangers, a musically diverse outfit plugged as a hillbilly band, debuted in 1932 as an amalgamation of KMBC musicians and performed on local and CBS series for twenty years as well as appearing in films and on television. The Rangers' fiddler, Gomer Cool, hired by Church in the late 1920s, was talented enough to strike out on his own during World War II and develop a solo career authoring dramatic scripts for CBS. Another musical ensemble, the Musical Masseys, honed their radio skills with Church and went on to a distinguished radio and recording career in Chicago and New York as Louise Massey and the Westerners.

Paul Henning may actually be the most famous employee that used KMBC as a stepping stone to brighter days, though his fame would come with television not radio. A writer and performer in the late 1920s and early 1930s for Kansas City audiences, he moved with wife Ruth to Chicago in the mid-1930s and started writing for *Fibber McGee & Molly*. He relocated to Los Angeles when the series left Chicago for warmer climates and found steady work in radio and later television. Henning left his mark in the annals of entertainment creating *The Beverly Hillbillies* and *Petticoat Junction* and contributing to *Green Acres*.

Women on KMBC

By the time Caroline Ellis became involved with Arthur Church and KMBC, the station already had women working in a wide

Aubry Waller Cook. From author's collection.

variety of roles, both on the microphone and off. They were most frequently hired as musicians and actresses but on occasion as writers. One of the earliest female musicians to earn credited airtime on the station was Aubry Waller Cook, a pianist who joined the staff in 1927 and focused her broadcasts on classical music performances on such programs as the imaginatively named *Classic Hour* (ca. 1930).

Gladys Smith, "the Pickwick Girl," sang as one half of the North-Mehornay Newlyweds and Dwarfies Harmonizers on different nights, but primarily as the second half of the Songsmiths, a husband-and-wife duo also featuring Woody Smith ("the Ozark Rambler," a nickname later passed on to Ozie Waters) who doubled as station announcer. Married in 1928 and first appearing on the air over Minneapolis' WCCO, the couple joined KMBC in 1929 and

Louise Mabie Massey. From author's collection.

specialized in more easy listening fare with piano accompaniment. A third less prominent female singer was Ruth Royal, a vocalist advertised as "The Girl of a Thousand Voices" who had solo broadcasts as well as airtime with other station musicians including the aforementioned Texas Rangers.

Without a doubt the most famous female musician to come out of the station's ranks was Louise Mabie Massey, a member of the group now remembered as The Westerners. Born in Texas, Louise grew up in Roswell, NM, where she began performing with her father and brothers. Premiering on radio on what was described in 1930 as a forgotten and shuttered New Mexico station, the ensemble made a brief stop in Topeka, KS, in 1929, and began appearing over the airwaves throughout the region on KMBC by 1930. Louise's husband Milton Mabie had joined her and brothers Curt (often called "Dott") and Allen by that time and when the Massey's father and patriarch Henry returned to New Mexico, Lawrence "Larry" Dilworth Wellington – more often known as "Duke" Wellington – replaced him on the accordion.

Louise was rarely, if ever, known by that name on KMBC, instead going by the moniker Velma. Not yet the Westerners, the quintet could be found across the station's schedule, often under the name The Musical Masseys, but sometimes as members of other station house bands including the long running Texas Rangers. Like most all KMBC staff, the musicians had non-performing duties as well, Louise's mostly being to act on the station's central show, *Happy Hollow*. Louise played Widder Jones Blackstone for the series during her tenure at the station. In 1933 the Masseys (plus Wellington) pulled up stakes for Chicago (as other KMBC stars would over the years) where they expanded their audience on WLS' wildly popular *National Barn Dance*.

Aside from music, women were most notable on KMBC programming via their roles on the station's homemaking shows and original dramatic and comedic broadcasts. The station's flagship *Happy Hollow* program served as the primary outlet for their acting talents. In addition to Louise Massey discussed above, nearly another half-dozen women have been individually identified.

Josephine Parshall in costume. From author's collection.

One was Josephine Demaree Parshall who recalled trying out for a job on a dare from some friends. Much to her surprise, Parshall was hired and played a regular character, Aunt Lucinda, on *Happy Hollow*. She also penned a weekly (later monthly) advice column for the station's newspaper, *The Happy Hollow Bugle*, in character. A native of Lathrop, MO, Parshall graduated from a local college and taught first grade at the town's elementary school until 1925 when she married Robert Parshall. The newlyweds soon moved to Kansas City where they resided for the next twenty years before moving to St. Petersburg, FL, in 1945. Parshall died of unknown causes a short time later at the age of 45.

Mondane Phillips Halley, who was married to Dr. George Halley, a fellow KMBC employee, toured the vaudeville circuits in the early 1900s, earning some attention for her songs and impersonations as "The Girl with Many Voices." An accomplished actress, Phillips was touring as far afield as New York by 1911. She is known to have played at least three characters on *Happy Hollow*, Mary Ann Fullerton, her mother Fanny Fullerton-Jackson, and Evangeline Adams. The character of Mary Ann proved popular enough to earn appearances on KMBC outside *Happy Hollow* including on her own shows. A girls youth organization, The Camp Fire Girls, sponsored Phillips' Saturday morning broadcast while her Thursday juvenile program attracted various sponsors during its run. They were regular features on the station during the early 1930s and earned some desirous attention from an advertising representative as related in a 1931 communique. One James Stickney of Ferry-Hanly Advertising Company happened to hear Phillips speaking to a colleague

Mondane Phillips. From author's collection.

while he was visiting KMBC. Immediately recognizing the voice, Stickney was stunned to see its source. Almost immediately he contacted representatives of the agency's Chicago and New York offices, encouraging them to look into Phillips' Mary Ann.

One of Phillips' specific series, aired 1932-1933, was *The Mary Ann Boy Scout Radio Program* which was heavily promoted by the city's Boy Scout associations. Her popularity seems in doubt in retrospect, with records indicating she averaged just under ten letters of fan mail per week.

At one point, Phillips went so far as to create a prospectus for a series featuring her "Mary Ann" character as the "Little Nature Explorer." It was to be a show featuring the "narratives of various animals" though not those found in the jungles for some reason. She emphasized the scientific accuracy of the program combined with simpler, child-appropriate language. To broaden its appeal Halley suggested covering child-friendly topics including dolls, flowers, insects, and toys. She also proposed an interesting feature-

Mildred Whiting. From author's collection. *Wretha Seaton. From author's collection.*

Virginia Harry. From author's collection.

within-a-feature, a serial entitled "The New Adventures of Nosey, the Mouse" that would be written into the Mary Ann scripts.

Mildred Whiting, a station stalwart until it was sold in the early 1950s and eventual wife of musical director P. Hans Flath, brought the character of Pay Check to vivid life in the *Happy Hollow* community. Wretha Seaton, a prize-winning reader and actress and pianist as a young girl in Wellington, KS, portrayed Kate Jackson on the show. Virginia Harry, who was singing on KMBC as early as 1928, played the character Margaret Watson by 1930.

Caroline Ellis was far from the first female writer to have original material aired over KMBC. Two women have been identified as having notable writing responsibilities for the station, primarily writing continuity, the industry term for what announcers read between programs and during nondramatic programs such as concerts and political broadcasts. One, Margaret Barnum, is primarily known via a handful of station publications ca. 1932 but is credited with early scriptwriting for *Happy Hollow*. A second, Ruth Lee Bren, was a seeming Jill-of-all-trades credited also with acting (*Happy Hollow*'s Sally Perkins), piano accompaniments, and stenographic responsibilities.

Homemaking on KMBC

Perhaps no station figure was more of a precursor to Ellis' quarter-century career than Lenore Anthony (d. 1970). A graduate of Lindenwood College ('09) in St. Louis and the Kansas City Conservatory of Music, literary pursuits were a primary interest for Anthony as a young woman. She founded the Lindenwood College Club in

Ruth Lee Bren. From author's collection.

Kansas City in 1911 and spent much of the 19-teens on the Chautauqua circuit as it hit its peak, booking shows and performing for Charles Horner of the Redpath Bureau.

Anthony periodically hosted meetings of her alma mater's Kansas City College Club at her house, which from 1925 to the early 1930s doubled as the Lenore Anthony Theatre Craft School. During this time Anthony also worked as Teacher of the Spoken Word at the Three Arts Studios where she taught classes to correct stammering and improve children's expression, as well as dramatic art classes in the evening. Anthony earned extra money giving talks on modern plays, drama, and storytelling.

Anthony was a regular on Kansas City radio as early as 1924 with WHB and is credited in some sources as the first sponsored female broadcaster in the city. Her earliest work was with discussion shows

Lenore Anthony. From author's collection.

such as League of American Pen Women, a civic club in which she was very active, even holding office as vice-president in 1922, and educational broadcasts including *The Book of Knowledge*. Upon moving to KMBC years later Anthony expanded her on-air duties to include both acting and homemaking commentary. She portrayed different characters on KMBC's *Happy Hollow* including Aunt Hattie and Anastasia White and also led programs of her own. One, *Lady of the House*, was a typical program in the homemaking genre that focused on cooking while others were more highbrow, including *Junior Artists' Club* and *Bits from the Classics*. In 1928 Anthony had a short book of poetry published by Kansas City's Lowell Press, simply entitled *Whimsies*.

On July 1, 1930, Lenore Anthony's *Lady of the House* program debuted over KMBC, and is recognized as the closest predecessor to Ellis' work that was to be found on the station. Airing at 11:15 on weekdays and 8:45 on Saturday mornings, the program opened with Anthony's folksy welcome: "It was only a glad 'Good Morning' as she passed along the way – But it spread the morning's glory, Over the livelong day." The style and content would prove to be only faintly like Ellis' early work on the station. While sharing and discussing recipes from ice box ginger cakes to barbecue sauces to tomato salads was central to her broadcasts, Anthony held various contests and offered prizes such as a Victor Superette radio and $45 in gold. She offered quilt patterns to her listeners as a way to measure audience size. In addition to sharing recipes Anthony recited homely verse and bits of music. Whenever possible she also liked to have female speakers on her program to talk on topics of interest to women. Among them were Elma Eaton Karr who talked on the subject of quilts, Dr. Mary Lower about summer anxieties, Naoma Andrus on "Women and the Economic Situation," and Dr. Mary Zercher concerning posture and its effects on disposition.

Scripts for *Lady of the House* no longer exist but a sales proposal and her columns from a station periodical provide insight to the tone and content of Anthony's broadcasts. In a promotional piece written when the KMBC team was attempting to lure an advertiser for the show, it was stated that each episode included two – and only two – recipes, both of which were either very old or very new. It also noted that over 1,800 copies of a Christmas candy recipe and 500 copies of salad dressing variations had been mailed out to inquiring listeners in recent weeks. The program's music was handled personally by the station's musical director P. Hans Flath.

An October 1932 column provides a taste of Anthony's tone and speech to her fans:

> There are few party occasions during the year that lend themselves easily to entertaining children as Hallowe'en. Grinning pumpkin heads, apples strung on cords, sheets converted into spooks, transform the most sedate living room, or the simplest basement playroom into the proper sepulchral background for such a party.
>
> An interesting game is played by providing each child with a thin bar of milk chocolate. In the center of the table have small cookie cutters shaped like pumpkins, oats, and witches. Ask the children to cut their chocolate bars with these – the child who gets the greatest number of figures from his bar wins a prize.
>
> Refreshments should be simple. Creamed chicken on toast, surrounded by a ring of green peas might be the first course. Dessert should be a huge chocolate loaf cake, frosted with chocolate and decorated with Hallowe'en symbols. Bake in the cake enough tiny fortune telling favors so that each child will find one in his piece. They can be wrapped in thin waxed paper before being stirred into the batter. Serve cocoa, topped with a marshmallow cat, with the cake.

Hallowe'en Cake
1 ½ cups flour
3 teaspoons of baking powder
1 cup sugar
1 teaspoon salt
1-3 cup cocoa
½ cup butter, melted
2 eggs
1 teaspoon vanilla
milk

Sift the dry ingredients into a mixing bowl. To the half cup of melted butter add the egg yolks, and then fill the cup to the top with milk. Beat this mixture thoroughly, and then add the vanilla. Add this to the dry mixture and beat again. Finally beat the whites stiff and fold them into the batter. Bake the loaf in a moderate oven (350 F.) for one hour. When cool frost top and sides with fudge icing.
Sincerely yours,
Lenore Anthony

During her quarter hour Anthony sold her sponsor's goods, from evaporated milk to corsets to moth cakes. The devotion such broadcast formats could earn from listeners can be hard to fathom but was real nonetheless, as is illustrated by the following fan letter received from a Mrs. P. J. DeLaney of Kansas City in 1932:

Dear Miss Anthony:
When you are off the air for a day, I realize just how much I miss your program. You always give me an inspirational tho't as well as a valuable household hint or recipe.
Your readings in character or dialect are particularly entertaining and hope you see fit to give more of them.
Yours very sincerely,

Anthony's time after her years at KMBC remains a mystery for the most part, though it is known that she ran a new school for the arts in Kansas City in the early 1940s. She eventually married and today Lindenwood University offers the Lenore Anthony

Borgeson Scholarship. Station records suggest that even during her tenure on KMBC, management was continuously looking for new talent to either supplement Anthony's on-air material or replace her should the need arise. A show proposal that fit neatly into the genre personified by *Lady of the House* remains in the station's historic holdings.

Submitted in the early 1930s by one Hester Burgess Miller, a sample script for a proposed program called, interestingly, *My Lady of the House* reflects the quickly solidifying conventions of homemaking broadcasts. It was to feature "Dolly," described as a "bride-to-be" who was eager to provide household hints to her potential Midwestern listeners within a semi-dramatic monologue format. Perhaps reflecting the low regard in which these shows were often held, this proposal was actually considered "fairly good" by the station's staff member charged with evaluating new concepts. The reviewer only noted that some musical interludes would help break up the "large ... amount of straight talking" and be more appealing to listeners.

Of note was that even smaller regional stations like KMBC in the early 1930s were well past the period during which nearly anyone could walk in off the street and get serious consideration for a broadcast, if not an air slot, right away. Though not having any radio experience, Miller had domestic science coursework in college, sales experience in a dry goods store, and published writing with various newspapers including the *Journal Post*, the *Kansas City Star*, the *St. Louis Times*, and the *St. Joseph News-Press*.

Even so, Miller's work did not ultimately find a spot on KMBC's schedule, perhaps because of the stiff language in passages such as: "Now, little green diary, I'll start with you ... (I'll write in the red one tonight, for I will see Jack this evening, and I'll confide all about it to you), so here goes the green one." Or "Mother always rolls her [eggplant] with the rolling-pin, but I think I shall use the grinder. And then she fries them in hot lard, and that's all," a recipe that lacks the folksy charm expected of the genre and specificity necessary for listeners to replicate in their own kitchens.

Return to Kansas City

After five years away from Kansas City, Ellis returned in 1928. Her years with Hudson's and Crowley, Milner and Company in Detroit served her well and she easily slipped into a similar position with the Jones Store of Kansas City. Even the 1929 stock market crash and subsequent onset of a world-wide Great Depression could not dampen her growing career trajectory. Ellis quickly earned the title of Education Director for the Jones Store and in 1930 she was promoted to a buying position for the ready-to-wear department. There seemed to be nothing but blue skies ahead when Ellis was hit with yet another family death. In 1931, three years after Ellis left Detroit her beloved sister Gertrude died at the age of 49. Her husband and her son, Crockett Mosshart, both remained in Michigan and eventually her son married and raised his own family there.

While not as awe-inspiring as the 33-story Hudson's in downtown Detroit, the 12-story Jones Store that occupied a full city block – 12th to 13th and Walnut to Main – was a local institution and well on its way to becoming the largest department store in Kansas City. Within a year of returning to the City of Fountains Ellis reconnected with old friends, notably Rev. Burris Jenkins, and was promoted yet again at the Jones Store to a higher purchasing position in which she chose not only women's items but men's clothing including suits and coats. Unbeknownst to her, just as Ellis was settling in to a comfortable career with the growing department store in 1932, E. A. Warner, an account executive for Ferry-Hanly Co., was approaching the staff of KMBC to discuss some merchandising ideas.

Joanne Taylor's Fashion Flashes

When Warner approached Church's staff on behalf of John Taylor Dry Goods, Co. about creating a program to market the dry goods retailer, as outlined above Church had a pool of talented musicians, writers, and actors from whom to draw. But he didn't turn to any of his staff who had been proving themselves on the airwaves for the last five years. Instead, he heeded a suggestion offered by a local minister: Burris Jenkins. How the two men were acquainted is not known, perhaps just through interactions via their respective jobs. Regardless, Jenkins jumped at the chance to introduce his old friend Caroline Ellis to the radio executive.

Arthur B. Church immediately saw potential in Ellis, especially with her years of retail experience, and directed station vice-president Roland Blair and KMBC sales director J. Leslie Fox to put her in the forefront of the John Taylor negotiations. Talks were ongoing in 1932 and into 1933 as Blair used every strategy at his disposal to sell the retailer's vice-president H. Kenneth Taylor and treasurer and general manager Fred M. Lee on Ellis' credentials. It was a hard sell as the John Taylor Dry Goods, Co. was essentially being asked to finance a brand new show with no built-in audience in an unproven format to be written and headlined by Ellis who had limited commercial writing credits beyond a newspaper column and absolutely no experience of any kind in the radio industry.

Blair eventually prevailed and an initial deal was struck whereupon Ellis signed her first employment contract with Church. Effective May 1933, she received no less than $30 per week to "write, produce and take the part of Joan Taylor in the radio act known as 'Fashion Flashes'." Ellis immediately set to work creating the program that would reach the airwaves as *Joanne Taylor's Fashion Flashes*, though not without considerable input and direction from station staff.

A yellowed document from MacBride, Ullman & Ryder, Inc. that has survived since its receipt in July 1931 amongst mountains of KMBC records, strongly suggests where the station creators got their inspiration for Ellis' inaugural program. The agency attempted to sell KMBC's director on a women's interest series tentatively called *Fashion*, featuring a Dorothy Truesdell. Truesdell, like Ellis, had significant experience working for major retailers including Amos Parrish & Co. and Macy's. The pitch from the New York agency may have struck the Kansas City radio men as just a bit much for the tastes of their many rural listeners, with its discussion of white sports dresses, Parisian white polo coats, and "swagger length" jackets. Truesdell's descriptions of Paris summers, New York stores, yachting parties, and country club dances would have been just a bit too foreign for Midwestern homemaker tastes.

The name *Joanne Taylor's Fashion Flashes* was clearly intended to remind the listeners of sponsor John Taylor and the format resembled that of a quasi-newscast overlaid with considerable commentary. Sadly, no scripts of this series remain nor any copies of broadcast episodes, and only one example of the series is extant, an audition record cut in 1939, well after Ellis had left the show. Various promotional materials provide some insight to the series' content, however. The Joanne Taylor character was portrayed as the listener's personal shopper making her way through the John Taylor Dry Goods store. Such shopping assistance would have been more familiar to audiences of the era and Ellis certainly would have dealt with personal shoppers on a daily basis while working for department stores.

Aiding Ellis on the broadcast were her secretary, the "sparkly-voiced" Miss Keller, Jimmy, a "wise-cracking" office boy, and Sam, an African-American porter "for comedy relief." Historical records don't indicate who played these other roles but they likely included at least some of the actors discussed earlier. Both Ted Malone and Hugh Studebaker were involved in about every aspect of KMBC productions and wrote and acted in most of its dramatic features. The porter probably was voiced by Eddie Edwards, a sound effects specialist who played a stereotypically buffoonish blackface character named George Washington White on *Happy Hollow* and many other broadcasts until that caricature style fell out of favor in the 1940s. The show's premise was simple: Taylor (Ellis) would talk to her staff members and customers who dropped in to the John Taylor Dry Goods store and comment favorably about different aspects of in-stock merchandise. She would also field phone calls from "customers" inquiring about particular products.

The dry-goods vice-president Kenneth Taylor remained highly skeptical of the entire endeavor throughout its development and right up until it premiered on the air May 1, 1933, at 10:00 in the morning, a prime spot for a program aimed at female listeners, especially homemakers. At best, Taylor hoped Ellis could maintain the company's market share in Kansas City. To his considerable astonishment Ellis, playing Joanne Taylor despite lacking even the slightest bit of acting or performing background, attracted new customers from 182 counties in Kansas, Missouri, and other surrounding states; new customers who specifically wrote to Taylor with their new business. Within three years customer charge accounts outside of Kansas City were four times their 1932 level.

Ellis' success came despite the fact that the John Taylor store rarely ran sales, a common tactic to attract business. Her discussion of a particular item on *Fashion Flashes* on numerous occasions caused a sell-out of that product in their store within hours of opening. At times Ellis was even given the unenviable job of moving clearance merchandise at the end of a season, when the products were no longer fresh. H. Kenneth Taylor again publicly sang Ellis' praises, marveling that she sold $700 worth of marked down end-of-season dresses in a single day. Retail knowledge gleaned from ten years in the department store industry and even more years of writing placed Ellis in a unique position to appeal to John Taylor's core audience.

In a presentation to the Advertising Club of Kansas City, Kenneth Taylor highlighted some other very specific sales data to demonstrate the power of radio advertising. Because the items in question were not promoted through any other avenues, Taylor could make direct comparisons in sales both before and after inclusion on *Joanne Taylor*. One new customer had traveled 175 miles to drop $85 at the store based purely on listening to the show. The store was now getting visitors from as far away as Denver. One mention of some silk robes in 1934 caused 80% of the garments to sell at full price almost immediately. Just a comment of some crocheted tams at full price increased sales to three times the pre-*Joanne Taylor* sales. KMBC and Caroline Ellis were spreading John Taylor's commercial brand far beyond the immediate Kansas City area, and increased sales more than made up for the cost of the series to the dry goods sponsor.

In October 1933, just months after the debut of *Joanne Taylor*, James M. Dignan of KHJ, Los Angeles' station in the Don Lee Broadcasting System, inquired to Ted Malone about "a department store broadcast" they had spoken of during an earlier West Coast trip by Malone. "This was a 'shopping Service' idea," Dignan wrote, "and as I recall, was most successfully used by a Kansas City

Department Store. If consistent, I would appreciate a case history of this account for presentation to the May Company here." To urge Malone into quickly providing the desired information, Dignan included an overview of a KHJ broadcast directed by the Dana Jones Agency for the Bullock's Department Store of L.A., in case it would be of interest to Kansas City officials.

Much to Dignan's chagrin an answer was slow in coming. Dignan wrote Malone again two weeks later after no response wondering "When am I going to get an answer to that letter I wrote you months and months ago in regard to the department store idea? I'm anxiously awaiting your word on this." It was yet another month before Malone typed out his letter, hemming and hawing about the delay and rightfully pointing out that KMBC management was reluctant to share details about *Joanne Taylor*.

Malone's superiors found it inappropriate for the station to share details of the program, instead encouraging KHJ to contact the *Taylor* sponsor, the John Taylor Dry Goods Company, directly about it. Malone's response offers one of the best first-hand accounts of the broadcasts and reflects KMBC's high regard for the talent of Caroline Ellis.

> The program is written and presented by a woman, Caroline Ellis, who plays the part of Joanne Taylor. The scene is laid in the personnel department of the store, and while the actual broadcast is from our studios, we endeavor to give the appearance of an actual broadcast from the store itself. The secretary is present, the stock boy, and some of the floor men and clerks. The broadcast is made up of fashion flashes, then conversations with various customers who either call on the phone, make a personal call, or who write to Joanne Taylor. She dictates the replies to her secretary, or she talks over the telephone, or she discusses it with the customer. It is just a little play – a dramatization of what might take place in the personnel department of that store. The advertising is worked into these conversations, and it is loaded to the gills; but it seems to be a very painless style of presentation.

Obviously, the weight of the idea is the personality playing the part of Joanne Taylor, but our lady seems to be putting it over in a big way. It's not only selling that particular client, but it's assisting us materially in making other sales alongside this broadcast.

The John Taylor staff devised an advertising strategy aimed directly at young child-bearing housewives using the marketing slogan "A step ahead on Petticoat Lane." *Joanne Taylor's Fashion Flashes* was moved on September 25, 1933 to 9:00 a.m., a spot identified as both the first "lull" in a homemaker's day and when John Taylor's front doors opened for business. To enhance Joanne Taylor's mystique the broadcasts were not opened to the public, at least at first, and the John Taylor store and KMBC offices made sure that Caroline Ellis was never available to take calls or answer questions. If an inquiry came into her during the broadcast a receptionist at the station or the store responded, "I'm sorry, Miss Taylor is on the air now. As soon as the program is over she will call you."

Taylor's doubts and his conservative hedge of only committing to an initial six-week trial run ultimately proved misplaced. The audience response was overwhelmingly enthusiastic and by the end of 1933 KMBC added a Saturday morning spin-off called *Joanne Taylor's Strolling Juvenile Players*. Using promotional material supplied by Bernie Bernfield, a United Artists publicist in Kansas City, a group of 9- to 12-year-old children put on a brief adaptation of a contemporary motion picture. Performed live at the city's Johnny McMaus Midland Theatre, the station even got permission from Walt Disney to include sketches based on their popular *Silly Symphonies*. *Juvenile Players* was replaced with a regular sixth daily episode of *Fashion Flashes*. After three years on the air H. Kenneth Taylor would say of Ellis' show: "[she was] friendly, casual, her remarks appeal to women because they strike a responsive chord in the mood of most women at that hour . . . Miss Taylor squeezes the last ounce of drama out of every line of her script."

Years into *Fashion Flashes*' run a typical episode began:

"This morning, as on every morning for the past 13 years, John Taylor's bring you the Joanne Taylor Program, with

Preparing for Joanne Taylor's Strolling Juvenile Players, ca. 1933. The back of the photo is inscribed by H. Kenneth Taylor, "To that good old pioneer of the ether – May she always knock them cold – Cary Crockett Ellis." Courtesy Steve Crockett.

a quarter-hour of helpful information on clothes and homemaking. As we enter the personal shopping office this morning, we find two elderly gentlemen talking very earnestly about their granddaughter. No one else is in the office. Let's listen …"

As the episode got underway the dialog between the two old men showed their concern for some items of clothing a granddaughter wanted but that her parents had chosen not to buy for her.

> Wilson: When you was listenin' at the key hole to Marcia talkin' to her mother, what else did Marcia say she wanted?
>
> Smart: That's what I got down on this list. Everything she named. Here's the note. Oh, confound it, I haven't got my glasses on. Now where in tarnation did I put them?
>
> Wilson: Looks like spectacles on your forehead there, John. Can't rightly tell from here.

Smart: Humph. Spring coat. She kept goin' on about it bein' a shortie. Miss Howard seemed to understand what she meant.

Wilson: More'n I'd know. Go on, what else?

The back and forth readily set up the inevitable opportunity for Taylor to begin her sales pitch to the audience. Chatham Blankets of New York was very pleased in 1935 to receive a copy of *Fashion Flashes* in which their Specification Sheets were promoted by John Taylor Dry Goods. The Chatham executive wrote: "You have done a remarkably fine job in interpreting the idea behind Chatham Sheets in terms that the average housewife will understand and appreciate. It is singularly rare that a retail store sells a product in just the manner that a manufacturer wants, and this is certainly one of those rare occasions."

J. W. McDonald, Executive Secretary of the Presbytery of Kansas City, MO, lauded Ellis' work from the perspective of an educator as opposed to a salesman. Addressed to "Miss Taylor" because Ellis did not receive on-air credit under her real name, McDonald wrote:

> I have for several years studied the theory and practice of informal adult education. Your broadcast is one of the most effective examples of this kind of education I have found. You know how to make your appeal by suggestion, and by way of the imagination. We are slow learning that adults are influenced more by life situations than by formal instruction. I have advised a number of teachers and public speakers to listen in.
>
> You are also selling more than goods. Your listeners are exposed to a sane optimistic philosophy of life. You and those who assist you are to be congratulated.

Ellis created a winning program but did so in a way that didn't commit her to it indefinitely. She stayed with the show for three years before moving on to other broadcasts but *Fashion Flashes* remained on the air for at least another ten years. From 1936 to 1941 Bea Johnson assumed the role of Joanne Taylor who gradually came to resemble a mix of Emily Post and Dorothy Dix. In

1938 Johnson had a series of conversations with H. Kenneth Taylor about freshening up the Taylor character as the series turned five.

They noticed an increasing number of listener letters grumbling about aspects of the show that may not be as relevant to women with certain body types or personality quirks. The two decided to begin slowly expanding the scope of *Fashion Flashes* by using one episode a week (Saturday initially) to focus on issues of "charm and style." Hundreds of letters poured in to the station in response to the initial broadcast requesting the offered *Charm-Style* bulletin. John Taylor had to double its mail staff to accommodate the volume.

Rather than selling specific wares from the John Taylor stores, these Saturday episodes provided advice on issues of "physical health and exercise, diet, hair styles, and make up." Bea Johnson, in the guise of Joanne Taylor, subsequently would recommend certain colors and styles that emphasized a woman's features. Joanne Taylor's audience convinced the dry goods store to begin a "tired business men" service that reminded husbands and fathers of anniversaries and birthdays. Not only would they aid in finding appropriate gifts but would send flowers at no charge. Taylor would lead adult education groups, many of which involved at least one "field trip" to the nearby dry goods store where she could answer specific merchandise questions, discuss displayed items, and share general housekeeping tips. Taylor's popularity was such that she was booked once or twice each day leading these groups.

John Taylor's Dry Goods also found the character of Joanne Taylor invaluable in moving merchandise that had proven unpopular and difficult to sell. Renaming some Egyptian yarn curtains "coronation curtains," in hours she sold out the product that had been lingering too long in the drapery sections. Some pleasant radio sound effects moved a stock of expensive Indian bells that had up until then not been enticing to buyers. By tying bells to Christmas packages later in the year on the air, the store sold yet more bells, eventually being forced to buy every bell the company could find from distributors to meet customer demand.

In 1938, five years after *Fashion Flashes* premiered and by which time Bea Johnson had replaced Caroline Ellis on the show, the daily quarter-hour was regularly attracting between 45% and 55% of

Kansas City listeners and was voted the area's top daytime program in a poll conducted by *Billboard* magazine. Even in the mid-1950s *Joanne Taylor's Fashion Flashes* was still remembered in the trade publications as was Ellis' specific tenure in the title role.

H. Kenneth Taylor, Vice-President in Charge of Advertising for the *Fashion Flashes*' sponsor, addressed the value of radio advertising for his dry goods business when speaking at the 28th Annual Convention of National Retail Dry Goods Association in 1939. A 1938 radio survey John Taylor's had authorized returned "startling" results. The day of their special radio sale overwhelmed the company's switchboard, prompting the telephone company to send over a technician to diagnose the trouble. Using the previous year's sales as a benchmark, sales from the radio special exceeded all company expectations considering a not-insignificant price increase over the prior year and generally poorer sales conditions. There was no question, then, that they renewed their sponsorship for a seventh consecutive year. In the late 1930s KMBC staff made efforts to syndicate *Fashion Flashes* with an eye to replicating the Joanne Taylor sales magic in other markets. Sample script packages were compiled as were transcription recordings that were subsequently sent to regional outlets and any others further afield expressing interest.

With new host Ora Howard taking the helm of *Fashion Flashes* in 1941, the series ran until after World War II. A fifteen-year run may not initially seem so impressive when compared to numerous network programs, from comedies to dramas to serials, that had been on the air just as long or even longer by then. But it was very uncommon, as professional insiders even acknowledged in 1946, for a local program to air so long under the sponsorship of a single local business without the financial backing of a larger national company.

The Travels of Mary Ward

While writing the original seasons of *Joanne Taylor's Fashion Flashes*, Ellis continued to write stories and poetry, a small amount of which has survived. Notations indicate a handful were published in the *Kansas City Post*, possibly when she contributed pieces under Burris' leadership in the early 1920s, but possibly during the early-to-mid-1930s as the newspaper (since renamed the *Kansas City*

Journal) and the radio station had a cozy relationship. The *Journal* regularly featured previews, reviews, commentary, and advertisements for KMBC programming. A very few of Ellis' poems even found their way into KMBC publications such as *The Happy Hollow Bugle*, a weekly (later monthly) newsletter mailed to subscribers that talked about the goings-on at the station. One such poem was included in the July 1933 issue after its inclusion in a recent episode of Ted Malone's *Between the Bookends*.

> The Breeze
> Just now a little breeze came wandering in
> Between the curtains on my window sill
> A little fragrant, vagrant Southland breeze-
> It sought my face and wandered o'er my brow,
> Lifting the damp hair on my temples; then
> It touched my eyelids, smoothed each cheek
> And laid itself about my throat
> In gentle, soft caress. All suddenly
> My mouth grows tender, round my lips
> There grows a wreathing, reminiscent smile,
> My eyes close down with dimmest memories-
> That little breeze is like my lover's hands.

In early 1936 Montgomery Ward hired the Ferry-Hanly Co. agency (which had previously brokered the deal for *Joanne Taylor*) to develop a program to promote the department store chain. Having experienced such success with Ellis, Ferry-Hanly's representatives didn't hesitate to approach Arthur B. Church about using Ellis to create a transcribed program to be aired over fourteen stations throughout the Midwest. KMBC staff agreed to terms with the agency and Ellis subsequently left the character Joanne Taylor that she had cultivated for three years to become the brand new Mary Ward. When the Montgomery Ward opportunity came along Ellis was hesitant because she had such a good thing going with John Taylor Dry Goods. But Midland Broadcasting executives applied some pressure and convinced her to make the change. Years later Ellis recounted that she could have stayed with *Fashion Flashes* as long as she wanted, as long as she could continue to write scripts and her voice stayed strong. In fact, she "had what amounted to a pension" working that show.

John Taylor, Jr., wrote a heartfelt letter to Ellis upon learning she had accepted the Montgomery Ward account.

> "I was delighted to receive your letter in one respect, in another respect I feel that we are losing one who has put over a job that I did not feel was possible. As you know when the Joanne program started, in my own mind, I felt that it would be impossible for anyone to write a broadcast that would keep the public listening to sales talk over the air as the majority of times they are seeking entertainment.
>
> "I want you to know that I feel you have done a wonderful job for us and I am not so sure that our broadcasts will be able to bring the results in the future that you have been able to show us in the past. I am delighted that you are going with Montgomery Ward at such a fine salary because it is for your own benefit and while I feel terrible that we are losing you I know that you have put your heart and soul into our work and will always be with us in any help that you can give us even in the future."

In the midst of Midland Broadcasting Company's negotiations with the Ferry-Hanly Company, Ellis renewed her employment with Midland with a standard five-year contract dated July 27, 1936. Among the job expectations laid out in the contract were "preparation and writing of script for use in radio broadcasts, the production of radio broadcasts, performance of characters or parts in radio broadcasts, preparation and writing of script for the making of electrical transcripts for broadcasting purposes," and "the making of broadcasts generally." In return she was paid $60 per week plus 66% of the "gross proceeds and revenue" received for her services by outside companies, though incentives brought that up to 75% for revenue above $1,000 per week and 80% for revenue above $2,000 per week.

In a decision she would rue, Ellis agreed to the contract's clause allowing Church to take a 33% cut of her salary from Montgomery Ward as he increasingly acted as an agent for his employees who were getting work outside the station. At the time 15% was a typical cut for an agent and 25% was not unusual if the agent had really developed the performer (which Ellis did not feel was the case). But 33% was unheard of; even Ellis' lawyer asked why she was agreeing to these terms. She responded that she didn't want to break with Church and that the fee was worthwhile to her in exchange for "the sense of security it gave [Ellis] to feel associated with [KMBC]." Ellis estimated that Church made $2,000 off the *Mary Ward* deal with very little effort on his part.

The episodes for the new series were recorded at the World Broadcasting Service's Chicago studios, the same studios the station had used in 1934-1935 to record *Life on the Red Horse Ranch*, a 65-episode transcribed series featuring the aforementioned Texas Rangers. Recording of *The Travels of Mary Ward* began August 7, 1936, and the first fifteen-minute episode premiered on August 24. The agency's initial order called for 78 episodes to be recorded, or thirteen weeks' worth of shows based on a six-per-week schedule. An additional 92 episodes were eventually produced, bringing the series' total to one hundred-seventy. While the entire run exists in an archival library, just under twenty episodes are circulating among old-time radio hobbyists as of this writing. Though it represents Ellis' earliest radio work aside from *Joanne Taylor's Fashion Flashes*, they are the only known recordings of her broadcasts readily available to the public.

One sample episode gives contemporary radio historians a glimpse into the format of the program. Characters include the title character Mary Ward, a boy named Clifford, a black-dialected porter named Henry (reminiscent of the Sam character in *Fashion Flashes*) who claimed descent from John Henry, an unnamed secretary, and unnamed male colleague. In the quarter-hour show Mary composed a letter to a satisfied customer promoting a contest and recommending some goods from the latest Ward's catalog. From the characters to the dialog to the overall style of the program, *The Travels of Mary Ward* was very much a rebranding of *Joanne Taylor's Fashion Flashes* with simply a focus on Montgomery Ward's catalog goods instead of John Taylor's store goods.

Ellis' Mary Ward was every bit the saleswoman that Montgomery Ward had hoped. Sales executives were practically beside themselves praising Ellis' acumen to the KMBC management. After being on the air for one month, a single announcement by Mary sold over 1,600 pairs of panty hose. Other brief announcements on *Travels* led to sales of 9,300 yards of the fabric percale and 7,200 towels. When Ellis casually mentioned a face powder, nearly fourteen thousand requests poured in for sample boxes. Surveys by the company indicated that listeners had increased their Ward's purchases nearly 150%. A series of a dozen announcements plugging the Ward's catalog resulted in almost 20,000 requests from new customers, more than half of which included actual merchandise orders. One Ward's announcement went so far as to proclaim that the resulting sales boosts from Mary Ward were such that the show only ended up costing Montgomery Ward

Ad from The Fairview Enterprise August 20, 1936.

Caroline Ellis as "Mary Ward," 1936. Courtesy Steve Crockett.

Caroline Ellis featured in Advertising Age News, 1937. Courtesy Steve Crockett.

$17.14. Payment plans in the Kansas City region jumped from 8th among Ward's payment plan regions to 2nd after six months. Two radio surveys showed that Ellis' *Ward* program drew between 44% and 68% of the listening audience in the Kansas City area. Contests received well over 100,000 responses, representing more than ten percent of the entire metropolitan area.

The Montgomery Ward contract expired in 1937 and was not renewed, a seemingly unexpected decision considering the financial success reaped by the store chain from the program. For the next year and a half Ellis' career at KMBC appeared in limbo and caused her no shortage of confusion. H. Kenneth Taylor had made it clear he did not want any other Kansas City-area sponsors using her on their show, perhaps afraid a competitor would leech off the local fame Ellis had built up while promoting Taylor. For several months Church wouldn't even attempt to sell Ellis to any potential advertisers, leaving her in a lurch as to where she should be focusing her efforts. After considerable arm twisting, Taylor was finally persuaded to okay Ellis' work with a grocer's account. Not satisfied, Ellis made the case that she should be allowed to seek a national sponsor if local sponsorships were going to be off the table.

Beulah Kearney

As it became clear that Caroline Ellis' success with her hybrid dramatized homemaking programs would sidetrack her from becoming a headline broadcaster for KMBC's women's programming, the station hired Beulah Kearney to fill that role. Unlike many of her predecessors, Kearney came to the job with notable achievements and credentials in the homemaking field. In 1934 Kearney was appointed the role of Food Conservation Supervisor by the state of Missouri, a supervisory position over the state's 100 canneries and 9,000 employees of the Federal Emergency Relief Administration (FERA) canning project. She was, in fact, the only woman to hold such a position across the United States. As part of the job Kearney was tasked with writing a food service column that ended up being syndicated in 125 newspapers across Missouri. Kearney followed this in 1935 by conducting more than 100 kitchen schools in Kansas, Missouri, and Oklahoma in cooperation with local newspapers. Her column, renamed *Beulah Kearney's Kitchen Hints*, spread to all these papers as well.

After two years with the government Kearney took a job with KMBC in 1936 as director of the station's *Happy Kitchen* show.

Kearney's sales prowess was attested to in a letter from Ted Skinner of the Calavo Subtropic Fruit Co.'s Los Angeles branch. The fruit distributor worked with Kearney to air the *Happy Kitchen* on Southern California radio for two days per week in February 1938. The very first week of the joint effort resulted in greater than expected demand for Calavo avocados and the company could not meet retailer orders and had to arrange for immediate delivery of 100 more crates. Calavo also received more than 600 requests for their Library of Calavo Recipes, pitched by Kearney on the shows.

Kearney was sponsored by Millers' Temp 'Taters on Thursdays in late 1938 from 2:00 – 2:30 and by 1941 Kearney had relocated to Chicago, as had so many KMBC alums before her, after some time trying to break into New York. Unlike some of those same alums, including Goodman Ace, she left on good terms with Arthur Church and management. NBC optioned Kearney through August of that year and she developed new programming ideas while making the rounds to directors and agencies trying to land a commitment. She expressed relief in a letter to Church that her *Happy Kitchen* show was in good hands with Ellis briefly at the helm back in Kansas City.

A trip to California, where she had spent years during her youth, in the autumn of 1941 led to some promising meetings and even calls for more formal audition material from some clients. Unfortunately for Kearney "NBC somehow never could get the salesman and the spot man together" and nothing concrete materialized. She also placed some of the blame on the increasing government attention to NBC's ownership of both the Red and Blue networks, leading to the distraction of Blue executives who otherwise might have been focusing on her show.

Not discouraged by the lack of action with NBC, after finishing a 90-day extension Kearney decided not to re-sign with the network and turned to selling her show herself. With only the income from a regular recorded spot to fall back on, she worked to arrange for future recordings on the West Coast for the time being. One of her first big prospects was with Calavo, the fruit distributor with whom she had worked in years prior. They were immediately interested in hearing a presentation for a California morning spot and also wanted to pursue talks about a seasonal spot for their Kansas City outlet. Just as federal attention to network monopolies put a brake on Kearney's work with NBC, so did the transferring of Calavo's account from Lord & Thomas to the J. Walter Thompson agency complicate and slow down discussions.

Ultimately, Kearney's West Coast stay was short-lived and within two years she was back in Chicago finding success with a daily program and weekly evening show as well. In what free time she had, Kearney continued to develop new ideas and get them on the air. Her services were in such demand that she found herself turning down contract offers, such as one from Swift for a daily show because she already had a year contract with the Maggi seasoning company. A subsequent letter written January 25, 1945, revealed her Christmas-day broadcast appeal for letters to be distributed to soldiers resulted in 2,314 pounds of mail delivered to the Blue Network's Chicago offices.

During 1945 Kearney was heard on *Meal of the Day*, a daily 25-minute food feature that aired on the Blue Network advertising Chef Boy-Ar-Dee's Spaghetti Dinner. At the peak of the show's performance *Meal of the Day* earned a 3.2 Hooper rating (meaning the percentage of radio sets tuned into the program), beating out the competition on the Red Network, CBS, and Mutual (2.1, 2.4, 2.3 respectively). The next year in 1946 the series was resurrected as a transcribed series of 5-minute episodes offered by Unusual Features Syndicate, the same outfit that produced *Incredible, But True*. Kearney's features were associated with a number of sponsors including Allsweet Margarine, Calavo Growers, Kellogg, Knox Gelatine, Morrell & Sons, Norge, Libby, McNeil & Libby, Peter Pan Salmon, Pillsbury Flour, Presto Cake Flour, Sunbrite, Sunsweet Prunes, Washington Apples, Westinghouse, and Wilson & Co. among many others.

Yet another series Kearney spent considerable effort pitching ca. 1941 was *The House of Heinz* to household goods producer Heinz. Like many homemaking shows, this series made explicit appeals to listener nostalgia and attempted to recall the "beloved memories of by-gone days." The proposal offered more than just the intimate voice of Kearney, however. She added an African-American caretaker, Ephrian Agnostatius Browne, for a "touch of humor and whimsey" and an unnamed secretary who served as a vehicle for bringing listener concerns to Kearney's attention.

Part 3: Big Time: Caroline's Golden Store

Caroline's Golden Store

Caroline Ellis' recent run under Ward's sponsorship convinced KMBC to see her as much a dramatist, both writer and actor, as a pitch woman. For a short time after the contract with Montgomery Ward ended she returned to local broadcasting, conducting human interest interviews and talks with housewives, county agents, and local agriculture leaders. At the time these broadcasts were little more than a way to keep Ellis busy while she turned her attention to her next big series and while Midland Broadcasting figured out a way to market her. The contacts developed during this intervening period, however, would prove valuable two years down the road.

General Mills, then a relatively new conglomeration of several small milling companies, was interested in sponsoring an Ellis-fronted show on a circuit of Midwestern NBC stations. This would represent Ellis' first network spot and a rare opportunity for KMBC to showcase its talent on a network chain. In the past, KMBC performers had primarily appeared on the smaller CBS network and rarely beyond its West Coast stations. Getting some attention on NBC offered big potential, both for Ellis personally and for Church and KMBC as a broadcasting business. A sponsored network show – on a network of NBC's Red series of stations no less – was the pinnacle for a radio performer during that era. With the food maker's backing, Ellis turned to creating her most visible project yet, a program which she felt bold enough to name after herself: *Caroline's Golden Store*.

Building on the successful formula she'd utilized over the past four years, *Caroline's Golden Store* deftly wove the company's advertising into the scripts, similar to the manner perfected by writer Don Quinn on the highly-rated radio comedy *Fibber McGee and Molly* and the style that years before had led to success upon success with *Joanne's Fashion Flashes* and *The Travels of Mary Ward*. Ellis

Caroline Ellis as Caroline of Caroline's Golden Store, ca. 1939. This shot became the most common picture of Ellis used in the press until her retirement in the 1950s. Courtesy Steve Crockett.

again played the namesake lead role, Caroline, who ran a general store in the non-descript small town of Arden. She was described as a "friend to everyone" and involved herself in the day-to-day dramas of friends, neighbors, and customers. Similar to the strategy Ellis used in writing *Mary Ward* in which she directly pitched Montgomery Ward products within the story, the Golden Store sold goods marketed by its sponsor General Mills. Caroline had the uncanny ability to identify the perfect General Mills item to meet every need of her community. Undoubtedly her father's years of running a small general store also gave her unique insights to writing about the proprietor of such an establishment.

General Mills initially had doubts about its new series as Ellis' scripts began to reach the home offices in Minneapolis. The longwinded introductory and closing commercials that were common on the daily serials the food manufacturer regularly sponsored were dispensed with in Ellis' proposal. In their place was more subtle advertising expertly interspersed into the script of the program itself. Despite these doubts, General Mills executives were hard pressed to overlook Ellis' record of building brand interest and *Caroline's Golden Store* finally received the green light to go forward with a six-month test run to promote Gold Medal Kitchen Tested Flour. Beginning August 15, 1938, *Caroline's Golden Store* would be broadcast from Des Moines' WHO. Unfortunately, there are no clues suggesting why WHO was chosen as the originating station for the tryout. It certainly makes sense that a sponsor would want to work the bugs out of a new series before launching it from the Midwest's radio center, Chicago, and WHO was geographically midway between Kansas City and General Mills' home outside Minneapolis. No less important was WHO's affiliation with NBC-Red, the intended network for wider regional broadcasting.

Ellis agonized over moving to Des Moines for the debut of *Caroline's Golden Store* because it meant being away from Kansas City for thirteen weeks to begin, and with a successful reception an indefinite period of time beyond that. But the financial rewards were significant, with her various fees adding up to nearly $1,200 per week for the network show; Ellis decided the offer was too good to pass up. Used to a modest lifestyle, Ellis created a trust fund in which much of the income was placed. Years later a nephew recalled that at some point Ellis changed the trust's beneficiary from herself to her brother, whose family had times of real financial need. Unfortunately, when her brother died the company administering the trust fund kept the remaining monies, resources Caroline could have used in her own later years. After Ellis' contract had been negotiated, KMBC's Fran Heyser was subsequently brought on board for the *Golden Store* 13-week try-out. He received $25 per episode for directing the daily serial with an additional $6.25 added on for episode repeats.

While Ellis focused on the personal aspects of devoting herself to a show based so far from home, KMBC executives moved ahead developing merchandising ideas for the show. Among those suggested between staff were a *Golden Store* certificate that could be redeemed for Gold Medal Flour or other grocery products and a golden carrying bag given to buyers of the flour.

The legendary radio agency Blackett-Sample-Hummert was responsible for putting together the *Caroline's Golden Store* package for General Mills. Blackett-Sample-Hummert was the biggest single player in the soap opera market and was responsible for literally dozens of serials throughout the entirety of the Golden Age of radio. The agency signed a contract with Arthur B. Church on August 5, 1938. The Midland Broadcasting Company received $70 per quarter-hour episode for Ellis' services, $45 of that for her script and $25 for her performance. The acting fee grew 25% for a repeat performance. After one year that $70 episode cost was to increase to $100. While Midland Broadcasting was responsible for finding an approved replacement should Ellis be unable to appear on any broadcasts, she was considered an employee for tax purposes of the Hummert agency.

Ellis, who took up residence in Des Moines' Chamberlain Hotel while working on the show, penned a letter to Church on September 12, 1938, just a month after *Golden Store* went on the air. She was dissatisfied with the distribution of income from the show and her note revealed a sour turn in their relationship that took quite some time to eventually heal. Earlier that year in a meeting Church had shared with Ellis his thoughts about her place at KMBC after having the Montgomery Ward contract terminated the year before. While Ellis continued to broadcast for KMBC, it was in sustained spots, programming that was not sponsored and that did not provide revenue. In a manner she considered unnecessarily cold, he said, "It [would] be many weeks before we're in the black on Caroline Ellis." She was indignant:

"I had never thought of it that way. To me, I had an honest to goodness job. A very nice job, let us say, for Kansas City. I was doing my work as well as I could, asking for more, trying to make myself as important to the station as possible. It never occurred to me for a single second that I was living on borrowed money – money that I would be expected to return. If it had, I assure you I wouldn't have stayed a day. I would have gone to you at once upon the termination of the Ward account and asked for release from my contract. I have never in my life lived on borrowed money, and I don't intend to – knowing it. After all, while radio is pleasant – and working for KMBC pleasant, also – I can scrub floors and I'm a fine cook and perfectly swell dishwasher. And what I earned would be mine, and leave me under no obligation to anybody."

Church was quick to respond to Ellis' veiled threats to return to hotel housekeeping, recognizing her extreme dissatisfaction with the working situation. After reassuring his "good friend" of the full confidence he had in her, Church offered a sideways apology:

"A few years hence, when I have grown my white beard, I hope to have gained enough additional knowledge of human nature and how to work with people to know how to maintain perfect employer-employee relationships. In other words, I realize fully I have lots to learn on this all-important subject which has challenged economists and sociologists from the beginning of employer-employee relations."

Nevertheless, differences remained as to what percent of the General Mills' payment each party was entitled to and Church didn't want to respond to her proposal yet because he couldn't give it his full attention. But he did his best to reaffirm their professional relationship:

"As far as I am concerned, Caroline, I want you to forget about any differences of opinion concerning the contract and proceed with full knowledge that Arthur Church is not going to push you in any respect, but will be glad to discuss these matters with you at some time in the future when you feel like bringing up the subject. Arthur Church is sold 100% on the loyalty and honesty and friendship of Caroline Ellis."

The People Behind *Caroline's Golden Store*

The cast of *Caroline's Golden Store*, which aired every weekday in Des Moines from 11:15 to 11:30, included Cliff Carl who joined WHO in 1937 and played the show's Uncle Jim. A seasoned stage comedian, Carl also played Pappy Cliff, the barber and town constable of *Sunset Corners*, WHO's own Saturday variety show set in the small town of Sunset Corners. Carl was a regular on another regional daily, *Coffee Pot Inn*, sponsored by Butternut Coffee, on which he was part of a comedy team, McNutt and McNutt, with Shari Morning, another *Golden Store* cast member. He went on to appear in the subsequent Chicago broadcasts of *Golden Store* as well. Others in the cast were Sarabeth Barger, a raw talent who had little experience beyond reading advertisements, Maxine Gibson, Bill Kilmer, Gwen Anderson, and Jack Smith. Little else is known about these Iowa players beyond their appearance on this show.

Ellis' program was directed by Fran Heyser, an actor and dramatic coach who also was a long-time KMBC employee and who relocated to Des Moines with Ellis. Formerly a program director with the station, Heyser had more recently assumed the responsibility for directing national programming that was being produced by Arthur B. Church Productions, one of Church's radio-related business offshoots. Demonstrating their satisfaction with Heyser, Harry Y. Bingham of the Blackett-Sample-Hummert advertising agency that was in charge of placing *Caroline's Golden Store* for General Mills, signed a contract for the option to continue using his services for a year at $125 per week paid to the Midland Broadcasting Company.

When Heyser relocated to Des Moines for the initial thirteen-week run, J. Lewis Reid was hired as program director to take his place in Kansas City. Lewis was a true radio pioneer himself, reportedly joining Newark's (later New York City's) WJZ in 1922 for announcing and acting duties. In 1929 he moved to WOR

Director Fran Heyser. Courtesy Steve Crockett.

and then WMCA where he was named program director before resigning in 1935 to work as radio director of the William Rankin advertising agency that produced a number of programs for Standard Oil. After a move to the Schillin Advertising Agency in 1936 Lewis was fired and subsequently hired soon after by KMBC.

In addition to directing *Caroline's Golden Store*, one of Heyser's primary responsibilities seemed to be keeping Ellis' temper in check; the slightest Hummert suggestion that a script could be improved led her to "hit the roof and [bounce] off of four mike stands." Heyser spent considerable effort reassuring Ellis that their wish for her to provide better character introductions was really a minor quibble, indicating they didn't have any significant issues with her work. Every day was potentially fraught with such incidents, however, since "saying anything about Caroline's scripts [was] just like slapping a child in front of its mother."

Even Ellis recognized her temper in this regard, though she placed the blame squarely on the agency representatives. Writing to a friend back home she explained that this was how the big agencies worked: the first month everything is just fine and one's writing is perfect; the second month they begin to pick at minor points and then by the third month, when a 13-week contract is up for renewal, "they wonder how in the world they ever hired you." She even conceded that in this one particular instance Blackett-Sample-Hummert was correct in asserting the introductions needed more work.

Cast and staff of Caroline's Golden Store broadcast from Des Moines in 1938, Heyser and Ellis are second row center. Courtesy Steve Crockett.

For six months, from August 15, 1938 until February 10, 1939, *Caroline's Golden Store* entertained daytime listeners of WHO. By January concern grew among Ellis, Heyser, and Church that General Mills was laying the groundwork to dump the program. Their liaison with General Mills, Mix Dancer, was continually enthusiastic about the program but as the new year opened he began to hedge his praise with warnings that money may run out and that while the home goods producer had budgeted money for the test run, funding for an ongoing commercial run was murkier.

It was at this point that the idea was introduced of wrapping up the current 13-week extension in February and resuming in summer when General Mills' new accounting year began. This distressed both Ellis and Heyser no small amount as they, both radio veterans, appreciated the time and effort that went into building a loyal program audience, an audience that could easily be lost should a show disappear for any length of time. Hopefully, they discussed with Arthur Church, expenses could be pared back to allow a leaner program to air into the summer when a new budget could be expected.

Such hopes dissipated in the face of corporate number crunchers and *Caroline's Golden Store* was not renewed for a third 13-week period in February. This was offset, however, by indications that General Mills planned to allocate money for a guaranteed one-year run to begin during the summer. Writing to Ellis, Mix Dancer did his best to highlight the upside of the situation:

> "Three Cheers – and I mean No Fooling!
>
> I know you and Fran felt disappointed at the moment that the show couldn't go on in Des Moines, but there were many things involved which made it impossible.
>
> The 26-week test was a success, so much so that we are going to give you a 52-week non-cancellable contract – the first of this kind General Mills ever gave any show. So they must think the show is going to do the job."

In addition to Dancer's enthusiasm, Harry Bingham – another Hummert executive – expressed in a January 1939 personal note to Arthur Church that this sign of confidence by General Mills bode well for everyone. That the company wanted to start the program with a 52-week non-cancellable contract meant, in effect, they were signing a two-year contract because "[Church could] be sure they won't stop after an investment of one year . . . the second year is really the beginning of returns on a program of this type."

Satisfied with the six-month test run of 130 episodes, General Mills allowed *Caroline's Golden Store* to leave WHO on February 10, 1939. General Mills followed through on Dancer's promises and authorized Blackett-Sample-Hummert to buy time on a chain of Midwestern NBC-Red stations beginning June 5, 1939. While many of the local Des Moines performers held out hope that the summer resumption would originate from WHO, and while Ellis enjoyed her time there well enough, she was quick to point out that Chicago was the place to make any real money in the business. If any of the actors hoped to really make a full career of acting, Chicago would be their best shot.

Soon after production ended in February, Caroline Ellis and Fran Heyser returned to Kansas City in high spirits, ready to spend the spring preparing for the program's summer return. There would be trips to Minneapolis to meet with sponsor representatives and Ellis was going to be required to have eight weeks of scripts finished prior to the show's debut. Incidentally, it was around this time that Ellis began intentionally trying to hunt down relevant newspaper and magazine clippings to create a scrapbook of her professional radio work. This scrapbook would fortunately stay in her family's possession, allowing a modern retrospective of her life.

During the months that *Golden Store* was off the air, Midland Broadcasting received $150 per week from General Mills to keep Ellis and her show on reserve. For the 10 weeks of summer broadcasts (June 5 – August 14, 1939) Midland received $350 per week for her work, a sum that grew to $500 per week beginning August 15, the one-year anniversary of the show, and $650 per week if it lasted into a third season that would start in 1940. The contracts also specified that the right to use Ellis' voice on any broadcast would be reserved solely for Blackett-Sample-Hummert.

Mix Dancer, a vice-president with the Blackett-Sample-Hummert agency, oversaw the signing of the contract with Arthur B. Church that took *Caroline's Golden Store* to Chicago. In the weeks between the Des Moines and Chicago originations, Ellis spent a couple weeks at General Mills' home office in Minneapolis getting acquainted with various executives and especially at the company's testing kitchen. There it was expected that she would get to know Marjorie Husted very well. Husted, of course, was the fictional Betty Crocker and virtual face of General Mills. She had radio experience in the homemaking field that stretched back nearly to the beginning of commercial radio and could initiate Ellis into both the food processor's culture as well as the ins and outs of aural homemaking.

Aside from the trip, Blackett-Sample-Hummert also wanted eight weeks' worth of scripts – forty episodes – completed before *Golden Store* returned to the air in June. By May 7, just a month before the show was scheduled to reappear on the air, Ellis had finished only two weeks' worth. Dancer threw in a suggestion that after Ellis was done in Minneapolis she should visit Chicago and meet with Dave Owen, the man in charge of General Mill's radio productions. It was Dancer's opinion that "[the Hummert staff] can be quite helpful to her, I'm sure, in plotting . . ." This suggestion for assistance writing the scripts was a minor point of that memo, and one that was probably not given much thought at the time. Nevertheless, it was a point that would return to the forefront later in the year.

Interestingly and quite improbably, both Church and Dancer had grown up in the small town of Lamoni, IA (population 1,541 in 1910) in the southwest corner of the state and had even been friends for a time. Fond childhood memories only added to the pleasure of both sides as the deal was finalized. After trips to Minneapolis sandwiched into their spring return to Kansas City, Caroline Ellis and Fran Heyser repacked their belongings and in late May relocated to Chicago for an indefinite future. Ellis took up residence at 1250 Stone St. from which she could see Lake Michigan. WHO's Cliff Carl who played on the original 26-week run, also moved with the program to NBC's Chicago studios at WMAQ where it aired as a part of the *General Mills Hour*. In celebration of the contract the Churches hosted a festive party for General Mills and Blackett-Sample-Hummert executives as well as the show's cast.

Premiering across the Midwest on June 5, 1939, a velvety-throated quartet crooned the opening to what would be Ellis' most widely heard radio words:

> There's a golden store of goodness
> In the heart of man
> It's a part and parcel
> of the happiness plan
> It is not the kind of treasure
> That you put away and hide
> To find it all you have to do
> Is look inside.

This was followed by announcer Franklyn MacCormack setting the scene for the new audience:

General Mills presents Caroline's Golden Store.

> The small town of Arden, county seat of Arden County, is bisected by a broad highway leading to Scott City, sixty miles away. On this highway on the edge of what has become in recent years a very attractive residential district deep in its setting of fine old trees is the home of Caroline Gordon. To this home Caroline came as a bride and though circumstances took her far from it at different times during her married life, when finally she was left a widow and on her resources she returned to it, as to a haven. Finding herself in middle-life forced to earn her own living, she cast about for the thing she could do the best. The result was that on the corner of her roomy grounds between two great elms there arose a small, modern and attractive building, housing what she calls her Golden Store. The reason for the name will be plain as events move forward. Golden Store for body and soul. We find her with her porter and helper Sam Jefferson about to begin what we hope will be her successful business career.

In a departure from many of her serial contemporaries, *Caroline's Golden Store* lacked the ubiquitous organ strains prevalent in the genre. Instead, the men's quartet opened the show and provided gentle transitions between scenes. Both Caroline Ellis and her namesake series received a glowing review by the influential trade magazine *Variety* just two weeks into the run:

> 'Caroline's Golden Store'
> With Caroline Ellis, Jack Brinkley, Frank Behrens, Barbara Winthrop, Joan Kay, Guila Adams, Cliff Carl, Ginger Jones, Harriet Widmer, Franklyn MacCormack.
> 15 Mins.
> Gold Medal Flour
> Daily, 12:30 p.m.
> WMAQ-NBC, Chicago
>
> (Blackett-Sample-Hummert)
> General Mills has another probable winning daytime strip script. Should prove a welcome relief from the flood of courtroom-and-murder strips. This one is calm and quiet, full of homey comedy and talk. It's a show built around quiet and restful people in a rather small town. Instead of shooting and divorces, there is just simple plausibility.
>
> Commercials are not pasted on to the two ends of the program as in other shows, but are woven directly into the conversation in script so that the plugs come as a surprise and before the listener can set up what has become an automatic defense against the sales talk.
>
> Show was originally tested in Iowa and is a product of Arthur Church's show factory down at KMBC in Kansas City.
>
> Entire action centers around Caroline's grocery store, which makes it a natural for the commercials to be fitted in painlessly.
>
> Lead is by Caroline Ellis, who also writes the show. She's got a lot of radio in her. Rest of the cast is competent, and with announcer Franklyn MacCormack coming through with able job.

Columnist Don Moore, writing in the June 23, 1939 *Radio Guide*, gushed about the show, though in a private letter Ellis hypothesized the write-up was more a result of Moore's friendship with announcer Franklyn MacCormack than anything else:

"Caroline's Golden Store" is open for business and business is looking good. This is a new NBC program that tells the day-by-day story of a charitable, though poor, middle-aged woman who manages a small-town store. Caroline Ellis writes the continuity and plays the central character. The cast includes Joan Kay, Jack Brinkley, Virginia Jones, Fran Behrens and others. And here's welcome news to many: The important job of narrator and go-between is handled by Franklyn MacCormack, and the task fits well the poetry-reader's intimate style. Right here let's offer a bushel of big, red, grade A apples to the "Golden Store" and to General Mills for working the commercial plugs unobtrusively but convincingly into the continuity. Hooray for everybody! If they'll just stick to that policy they'll not only win undying honor as valiant pioneers but they'll find it will sell Caroline's goods better than the vaudeville-barker announcements that have become radio tradition.

While Cliff Carl moved with Ellis and Heyser from Des Moines to continue on the show, the rest of the cast was filled with Chicago radio professionals. In line with the city's long-established reputation as the center of radio soap operas, many of the cast had extensive credits on serials. Jack (John) Brinkley had moved to Chicago in 1932 after several years on New England and New York radio and earned credits on a number of soaps including *Betty and Bob*, *Kitty Keene, Inc.*, and *Ma Perkins*. Frank Behrens spent time on two fondly remembered children's serials from the era: *Jack Armstrong, All American Boy* and *Little Orphan Annie*. He was also a regular on *Lorenzo Jones* and stayed busy acting into the television period. Barbara Winthrop had only recently taken a position with the radio department of Rogers & Smith in Chicago. Previously she had spent three or four years on staff at KMBC, primarily writing continuity but also reworking scripts for their *Phenomenon* show that was being syndicated nationally and producing *KMBC Magazine of the Air*. Before landing in Kansas City Winthrop had been employed at Houston's KTRH. She spent many years in Chicago radio but never broke into the top tiers of programming, appearing on shows such as *Calling Barbara Winthrop* and *Dorothy Dix on the Air*.

Joan Kay (real name Phyllis Stepler) was a child actor and dancer in the 1920s who matured into radio in the 1930s, mainly earning roles on serials such as *The House by the Side of the Road*, *Kitty Keene, Inc.*, *One Girl in a Million*, and *Arnold Grimm's Daughter*, among others. Guila Adams worked on *Arnold Grimm's Daughter*, *Kay Fairchild, Stepmother*, and *Those Happy Gilmans*. Cliff Carl, the WHO alum, would go on to appear on *Scattergood "Baines"* but later in the 1940s returned to Des Moines where he took over the *Iowa Barn Dance*. Virginia "Ginger" Jones was a busy actress on *Kitty Keene, Inc.*, *Backstage Wife*, *Portia Faces Life*, *Story of Mary Marlin*, and *The Carters of Elm Street*, among many others during her quiet but successful career.

Harriette Widmer had voiced Aunt Jemima but would stay busy on broadcasts including *Wayside Theatre*, *Guiding Light*, and *The Carters of Elm Street*. Franklyn MacCormack was an established voice in Chicago radio by 1939 having announced such series as *Easy Aces*, *Poetic Melodies*, *The Story of Joan and Kermit*, and *Woman in White*. MacCormack was a working radio man; never well-known but a respected professional until the day he died on the job in 1971. Whatever problems Ellis' new show would run into they could not be attributed to its cast, a veteran group of performers who had proven themselves in the big time of Chicago radio and worked together on various shows throughout the 1930s.

Within a month of purchasing the time on NBC, General Mills had contracted for a half hour of time on CBS' WBBM, from 5:00 to 5:30, leading to some speculation in the industry media that *Golden Store* was one of the prospective shows that would fill the slot. In fact, the program would remain on NBC for its first 13 weeks but was then switched over to CBS beginning October 9, 1939, to advertise Bisquick. A five-week layoff between the initial NBC run and subsequent CBS run, though not as alarming as the months-long absence from the air during the move from Des Moines to Chicago, was not appreciated by the cast.

First and foremost, Ellis was peeved to see her weekly earnings from the program drop from $500 per week during the summer back to $125 per week during the time off the air. She fought without success for at least $250 each week since it wasn't her fault

Behind the scenes picture taken during a broadcast of Caroline's Golden Store. Courtesy Steve Crockett.

Behind the scenes picture taken during a broadcast of Caroline's Golden Store. Courtesy Steve Crockett.

Behind the scenes picture taken during a broadcast of Caroline's Golden Store. Courtesy Steve Crockett.

Behind the scenes picture taken during a broadcast of Caroline's Golden Store. Courtesy Steve Crockett.

Behind the scenes picture taken during a broadcast of Caroline's Golden Store. Courtesy Steve Crockett.

Behind the scenes picture taken during a broadcast of Caroline's Golden Store. Courtesy Steve Crockett.

General Mills decided on the hiatus. Second, as with the spring layoff, she commented that "I do not feel that up to date I have had any kind of chance to show what we can do, or to gain audience. Radio listening is so much a matter of habit. Women turn to the same programs day after day and when you lose them it's danged hard to get them back." With the change in networks came a change in broadcast time, however, and many associated with the program would blame *Golden Store*'s new time, 5:15 p.m., for some subsequent problems.

Historical records indicate that by the end of 1939 executives at Blackett-Sample-Hummert and Midland Broadcasting were recognizing some disgruntlement on the part of sponsor General Mills and were pointing the blame primarily at Ellis. In a December 1939 telephone conversation Mix Dancer shared his blunt concerns with Arthur Church, concerns that had briefly surfaced while Ellis was preparing the first 8-week batch of scripts during the summer. While Dancer conceded that *Caroline's Golden Store* was just as good as her previous shows for sponsors John Taylor and Montgomery Ward, there was considerable concern that the daily scripts were not "carrying enough hang-over material" that gave listeners a compelling reason to return to the program day after day. Just as importantly, the agency was finding Ellis to be a very prickly person to work with and wanted Church himself, as her boss, to address these issues with her.

Dave Owen, General Mills' radio program manager, was having to spend too much time working with Ellis on her scriptwriting; they needed Church to convince her to make changes in her writing style. Ideally, Ellis would let Janet Huckins, a new, younger writer, assist her in laying out storylines and developing some cliffhangers. Huckins was wowing everyone with her work on *Arnold Grimm's Daughter*, the General Mills program preceding *Caroline's Golden Store*. Pressed on other aspects of the show, Dancer admitted that producer Fran Heyser "[was] no genius [and would n]ever do any big production work in this town." Primarily, however, the discontent he was hearing grew from a need to get more "story value" for the sponsor.

Ellis, naturally, disputed some of the criticism. She complained that the General Mills executives had a practice of assigning different staff to listen to their shows every day and then report back with their thoughts. Being a serial with ongoing storylines, she argued that it was unreasonable to expect that anyone could tune in to just a single episode and grasp all that was going on. It was a criticism with which Owen agreed but had no power to affect. Ellis also rued having earlier praised Huckins' skills to her superiors as much as she had, especially, in retrospect, at her own expense.

Ellis had her own issues with the sponsor's management, even as they were applying pressure on Ellis and Heyser. While able to stay six weeks ahead in her script submissions as required, General Mills constantly infuriated her by asking for script changes involving new product promotions. Having to go back and essentially rewrite entire scripts from scratch that had been sent over by Ellis days earlier led to unladylike swearing in more than a few communications. She was regularly working until midnight to keep up on the show and these rewrites only added to her already long hours.

These pre-holiday rumblings went unresolved, however, and by February 1940 everyone involved with the show knew some changes needed to be made. In a confidential letter to Arthur Church, one of Midland Broadcasting's main sales executives, George Halley, reported back on his meeting with Ed Smith at General Mills' home office. Their meeting was completely unofficial as all radio business was supposed to be run through the Blackett-Sample-Hummert agency. Halley outlined some of the primary concerns Smith was hearing from co-workers.

First, the commercials that were worked into the script needed more variety. While their inclusion within the story at first had an air of novelty, now whenever the phone rang at the Golden Store listeners knew a sales pitch was coming. The following exchange from the second episode was typical of the format:

> "Today, business in the Golden Store is flourishing and we find Caroline on the telephone. Let's listen:
>
> You say your rolls weren't nice? (Pause) Oh, I see. (Pause) Well, uh, now you know Mrs. Mitchell, the flour has a lot

to do with that. (Pause) Yes, yes, some flours just don't rise as well and there's a certain tastelessness and flatness about the things you bake. (Pause) Yes, that's right. Nothing is as important in baking as the flour you use. Why don't you just try Gold Medal? Just get a small sack and try it once. I just believe you'll never have any more trouble. (Pause) Yes, I know, but you see, often times flours aren't the same sack after sack. You'll have success with one sack and then fail with the very next one. (Pause) Oh, yes, I used to have so much trouble that way in the old days, before I used Gold Medal Kitchen Tested. (Pause) All right, do that. I'll send just the smallest size and you'll give it a fair trial. You see I'm so confident of it that if you aren't satisfied I'll take it back and return your money. (Pause) Well, anyway, that's my guarantee.

(Sound of door opening) Oh, hello Uncle Jim, sit down.

Now, have you got yeast? (Pause) Well, I'll put in a cake. And say, Mrs. Mitchell, there's a folder of Betty Crocker's recipes in the sack and if you want to vary your hot bread that you folks all like so well, try that one for potato muffins. (Pause)

Mmm, mmm they're good. I had some for supper last night. (Pause) All right, now just as soon as Sam comes back and thank you Mrs. Mitchell and let me know how you get along with the flour. Goodbye.

Exacerbating the show's rut was the fact that Ellis refused to make certain accommodations to the sponsor's wishes. For instance, she absolutely would not allow her character – the lead character of the program – to leave the store. "Utterly silly," complained one executive, and it greatly hampered both story possibilities and the ability to have other characters deliver the commercial. There were a lot of options for freshening up the sales spiel but it seemed to Halley that Ellis was "obviously jealous of anyone else giving [the commercial] and tries to keep it all to herself. She's afraid of the other characters selling ability – afraid she'll be displaced."

Other writing concerns revolved around the recaps, a staple of daily serials that brought the listener up to date on prior episodes. In Ellis' case the issue was more a problem of a lack of recaps than the content of the intros themselves. She liked to begin each episode by setting the scene for the day's episode and jumping straight into the action; this was a direct result of a continued absence of meaningful continuity from episode to episode as had been raised back in December. Not only did this decrease the tension to bring back listeners, but new listeners had no idea what was going on since the announcer did not provide any backstory. Again, Ellis was a bit stubborn; she insisted that all her listeners tuned in every day and did not need such a daily introduction, an argument the sponsor found ridiculous.

Further, the scripts were greatly in need of more conflict. There were too many "sweet" and likable characters and far too few "villains." There flat out needed to be more action in the show and it was directly attributable to a lack of character conflict.

Caroline's Golden Store was receiving some other criticisms as well. Chief among them, and a serious detriment to any radio program, was ongoing complaints from employee listeners that they had trouble understanding Ellis' speech. "They find her diction faulty and hard to understand," Halley warned, characteristics completely unacceptable to any radio figure, especially the title character. He did note that Heyser's directing was making what few dramatic scenes found in the show too stilted, too old-fashioned, and too melodramatic. But Halley could address that directly with Heyser. Finally, while mention had been made two months before in regards to Ellis' lack of interest in accepting input and help from fellow writer Janet Huckins, the pressure was growing on Church to come right out and tell Ellis that she had no choice but to accept that Huckins was going to be essentially a co-writer and that Ellis' fee for writing the program was going to be nicked.

Conversations on Midland Broadcasting's side suggest that there were too many executives from Blackett and General Mills sharing their opinions on the program but too few willing to actually voice the concerns and point to areas of improvement. Ellis pointed out to George Halley that she had continually sought feedback from Blackett-Sample-Hummert since the show first debuted on WHO but nary a word was said. Though she'd been submitting her scripts even earlier than required, both General Mills and Blackett-Sample-Hummert had checked them and never required anything more than the editing of a very few individual words during that time. Only once had she been asked in to a conversation about the show and that was purely to review technical aspects of General Mills' "baker policy." Up until this time no one had suggested the stories needed any change at all; even the agency's copy department had failed to provide any guidance, leaving Ellis to create all the advertising copy dialog herself.

One of the few bright spots from the early weeks of 1940 was a Hooper ratings report from some mid-January surveys. Halley reported that *Golden Store* earned a very respectable 6.7 share, a gain of 3.3 over the previous month's report. While this trailed the daytime-leading serial *Ma Perkins* which garnered a 10.4 rating and the juvenile hit *Jack Armstrong, All American Boy*'s 9.8, Halley pointed out that Ellis' sponsor identification was extraordinary at almost 68%. It briefly boosted morale and when Huckins was officially brought on board as the plotter in February 1940, Ellis, Halley, and Owen all professed to feel that the ship had been righted and the future was looking up.

The reprieve was brief and by April tensions had resumed. The cast members started to openly question whether the show would even be picked up for another year and Ellis was increasingly reluctant to develop further storylines, insisting they had plenty of material to last until June when the contract ended. This chagrined George Halley to no end as he tried to lift everyone's spirits and encouraged Ellis to think more positively about getting renewed. As she approached her 63rd birthday, Ellis appeared ground down by the experience of writing a daily network show. She was "showing her age," Halley admitted, and undoubtedly was wondering if working at the highest levels of radio was worth it.

Week after week as the spring wore on the future of *Caroline's Golden Store* was looking increasingly precarious. Despite ongoing (and unwanted on Ellis' part) assistance from Huckins, Ellis had not made the script and store changes desired by Blackett-Sample-

Hummert. General Mills ultimately proposed an openness to continuing the show past the June 5th anniversary to July 19, but only if two conditions were met.

First, Midland Broadcasting had to agree to a price of $650 per week for a new year but only after a vacation break until October 7 at the weekly fee of $234. General Mills reserved the right to cancel the next season up until September 3. Second, and perhaps most contentious, the Blackett-Sample-Hummert agency insisted that Huckins be brought on in an official capacity to assist Ellis with all aspects of the writing. Additionally, Huckins would be paid 15% of the gross that was currently being paid wholly to Ellis.

The offered fees were not a problem for anyone because it was unquestionably better than the certain alternative of seeing the broadcast dropped altogether. Janet Huckins' status with the program was an entirely different matter, however. Ellis immediately objected to having Huckins officially assigned to the show and certainly to a 15% cut for her. There is no doubt Ellis wanted nothing to do with Huckins. In conversations she claimed that "aside from a few minor points, Janet has been of no help on the show" up to that point and, in fact, she felt "she must have more help than Janet [could] give her ... [Ellis] want[ed] a combination writer and secretary that she [could] have full time." She conceded only that she was open to sharing an office with Huckins where they could have "daily contact."

George Halley took exception to Ellis' positions. First and foremost, he flat out believed that Ellis "feared" Huckins and was intimidated by Huckins' capabilities. It was she, Halley argued, who had taught Ellis "how to construct an outline both general and weekly and how to work from it." The 15% cut was entirely too little; it should be closer to 25% for the "priceless assistance" Huckins had lent over the past several months for absolutely no additional compensation beyond her contracted salary. He was also very concerned that if the two shared an office Ellis would be "inconsiderate" of Huckins' time and not allow her sufficient focus to take care of her own show that General Mills was so eager to sponsor.

All parties involved in the show were in agreement to make General Mills' renewed sponsorship their number one priority, and the manufacturer's best offer of renewing through July and paying a vacation rate for some time after that was ultimately accepted. After some protracted wrangling the company agreed to a series of options on the show extending out five years with notable fee increases to $750 weekly until 1943 and $850 weekly until 1945. General Mills protected its own interests by maintaining the right to cancel at each 13-week interval with appropriate notice.

Caroline's Golden Store was extended about six weeks past its one-year anniversary and everyone involved with the program went into a summer break with no idea whether they'd be returning in October for a new season. Ellis put a happy face on and went ahead with outlining some stories (with Huckins' required assistance) to submit for Blackett-Sample-Hummert's review come fall. The last burst of optimism proved unfounded for all parties involved and on August 5, 1940, Blackett's Harry Bingham notified Arthur Church in writing that General Mills was cancelling their contract and forgoing all optional rights as of August 19, 1940. While there was disagreement among agency and station executives about whether General Mills truly did have budget problems or whether Blackett-Sample-Hummert simply got outplayed by a separate agency that was looking to poach the cereal company's advertising business, *Caroline's Golden Store* was off the airwaves regardless.

Ellis stayed in Chicago into October, working on prospective sales of *Golden Store* to new sponsors, none of which panned out. After cutting a series of sample announcements to try and sell to Sears, Ellis broached the possibility of returning to Kansas City permanently. Both George Halley, her main station contact in Chicago, and Arthur Church were delighted at this suggestion as they had already been discussing between themselves how to bring this up with Caroline. That she brought it up herself relieved them of some possibly unpleasant conversations. "If I went back to Kansas City, do you suppose they'd let me put on my chats to farm women again?" she had asked Halley one day. Church eagerly agreed and assigned Ellis to complete two audition programs in Chicago before returning home. One audition followed the *Golden Store* format while the second was more in the "chatty homemaker" genre.

Resettled back in Kansas City by November 1940 and once again wandering the familiar hallways of KMBC, Ellis was given a 1:00 – 1:15 slot during which she debuted a new show simply called *Caroline Ellis*. While keeping her broadcasting skills sharpened on the local homemaker program, Ellis spent time trying to build off her experiences with big-time Chicago radio and *Caroline's Golden Store*.

Lost Opportunities

Caroline Ellis wasn't ready to completely abandon the idea of finding success in the competitive but lucrative serials market. During the early 1940s Ellis developed three soap opera proposals that variously drew on her past serial productions, notably *Golden Store*, and her style of hybrid homemaker sales dramas honed on *Joanne Taylor's Fashion Flashes* and *The Travels of Mary Ward*. The series were *River to the Sea*, *The Marsh Family*, and *Wide Horizons*. Both *River to the Sea* and *Wide Horizons* received a heavy push in 1940 while Ellis was in Chicago wrapping up her time on *Caroline's Golden Store*. *Wide Horizons* was auditioned for numerous agencies during the year and *River to the Sea* was auditioned for companies such as Proctor & Gamble and National Biscuit Company (Nabisco) but neither was picked up. Less is known about *The Marsh Family*; there are no surviving references to audition recordings or broadcasts at this point but promotional materials were being distributed in 1941 so it was developed at the same time as the others. Internal Midland memos indicate that by the late summer of 1941 sponsor interest had waned in Ellis' audition series and that efforts to sell her outside the Kansas City regional area had slowed to a halt.

River to the Sea

River to the Sea remains a curious historical footnote as by many accounts and descriptions it is essentially *Caroline's Golden Store* under a different title. While it was very common for a program to change sponsors during its run, for a program to be rebooted under an entirely different name was more unusual and likely reflected either General Mills' ownership of the *Golden Store* moniker or a desire by Ellis and KMBC to distance their fresh sales efforts from any preconceived ideas about *Golden Store*. Business records are silent about the exact marketing decisions.

The title was inspired by "The Garden of Proserpine," a poem by British poet Algernon Charles Swinburne. Its second-to-last stanza reads:

> From too much love of living,
>   From hope and fear set free,
> We thank with brief thanksgiving
>   Whatever gods may be
> That no life lives for ever;
> That dead men rise up never;
> That even the weariest river
>   Winds somewhere safe to sea.

Ellis opened her new proposed series with the following introduction:

> Beyond all pain of living;
>   From hope and fear set free;
> We thank with great thanksgiving
>   Whatever gods there be,
> That even the weariest river
>   Runs somewhere safe to sea . . .

Names and places remained the same on the new series: the lead character in *River to the Sea* was named Caroline Ellis and was the same semi-autobiographical character as the owner of the Golden Store: "a middle-aged, childless widow, who lives in the home built by her husband when they were married . . . She was left some means by her husband but in middle life found this almost exhausted." Instead of entering department store sales, however, the fictional Caroline bought a small building in Arden where she became the proprietor of a neighborhood food shop. Getting rich was, of course, not important. Being a good friend and neighbor was all that mattered.

One promotion melodramatically set the scene: "An orphan girl, deserted by her husband, is sheltered by Caroline Ellis. Penniless, disillusioned, the girl discovers new beauty, new meaning in life through the love of a man willing to forget the past . . ." and suggested life-or-death storylines: "Flood waters swirl death and destruction along the riverbank. A capsized boat – a man and a woman struggling desperately to safety. A murderous battle on the lip of an overhanging cliff..."

Other characters were identical from the *Golden Store* scripts as well, including Uncle Jim Bentley, "the last of the 'city fathers' and a mentor to Caroline," and Mrs. Maria Crowley (likely in homage to former employer Crowley, Milner and Co.), Ellis' housekeeper. Crowley bears a crushing load, having lost three daughters to tuberculosis and enduring the trials of a "good-for-nothing" son. Caroline served as the matriarch of the town, as serial heroines were apt to do, and the 25-year-old Jane Darrell, a loner taken in by Caroline, served as the focal point for inevitable danger and unending travails. There were numerous stock good guys such as the wealthy socialite Ione Duncan, potential love interest and banker's son Dick Henderson, and bad guys such as the worldly and cynical Ronal Curtis, as well as the comedy relief of African-American characters, Sam Jefferson and Magnolia, who "stand by their 'white folks.'" The undated program outline includes two clues that the promotional materials used *Caroline's Golden Store* audience data to pitch the revamp. In the description of Uncle Jim Bentley it is noted that "scenes where he takes her [Caroline] to task have proved to be most popular to broadcast." Further, in Mrs. Crowley's overview it is mentioned that she is rearing the two children of her "good for nothing" son but that they "have never been brought into the broadcast." Ellis sketched out a number of speculative storylines involving dramatic courtroom showdowns and tragic suicide attempts, both common fare of the era's serials. Likely these would have been story kernels that were never developed during the original *Golden Store* run.

The Marsh Family and Wide Horizons

The Marsh Family was not a notably different program than *Caroline's Golden Store* and *River to the Sea* insofar as they were all middle-of-the-road melodramatic fare. The family drama, the title of which may have been intended to remind potential listeners of the popular *One Man's Family*, was filled with stock characters familiar from Ellis' other shows: Mrs. Caroline Marsh, "keenly intelligent" with an "appreciation of human values" served as the family matriarch. John Marsh, Caroline's oldest child, was a stoic 28-year-old who took over his father's role upon his death years before. John's bare education was made up for by his hard work and thrift which kept the family's farm solvent. Such untiring devotion to the family farm, however, kept his own outlook bleak with little hope of a different future. Lee Marsh, Caroline's oldest daughter at 20, longed for the glamor of the stage and was consumed with a life in show business at the expense of everything else going on around her. Twins Christopher (Kit) and Christina (Chris) were "young moderns" getting the education that eluded their older siblings. Finally, 14-year-old David, born just after the death of his father, is "studious, musical" and considered "a sissy" by some.

Set on the Marsh's family farm, *The Marsh Family* was the "story of men and women and children whose lives are bound up and sunk deep into the soil and what it produces and what it can be made to produce" and stories revolved around "the Marsh household and the contacts ... the clashes and the loyalties ... within the family, itself."

Ellis outlined a number of storyline ideas, giving prospective sponsors an idea of the show's potential direction and development. The Marsh's oldest son, John, balanced the needs of the family farm against his own desire to marry and begin a family with Jess, a nearby school teacher. Their marriage was all but a done deal in the eyes of the entire community. One of the twins, Christopher, while off at college and exposed to lesser elements, fell in with gamblers and found himself in debt. While seeking safety at home the entire Marsh family was drawn into his problems and John even used his life savings to bail out his younger and reckless brother.

Unable to remain in New York as the family money got tight, Lee (now Leigh) returned to the farm, resentful and bitter at the delay to her theater dreams. She brought with her Betty Ann, the show's "present menace," who had a low opinion of rural life. While she encouraged Christopher's affection, Betty Ann was secretly planning to win the older John's attention and break up his relationship with Jess. When mother Caroline Marsh moved to break up Betty

Ann's machinations, Betty Ann inserted a wedge been John and his mother and further stole a plum role right from under Lee's nose. Through all this twin sister Christina grew distant from the family while away at school.

The third of Ellis' serial efforts was *Wide Horizons* and departed from the patterns she'd established in her other work. This proposed series targeted young rural women who she dubbed the "modern generation." At its core the show focused on a young couple, Anne and John McMillan, and "their problems, aspirations, their fun, their failures, their love, courage, resourcefulness." Ellis cast her net wide in describing the show's undergirding theme: "the vast scope and on-goingness of nature. Birth and death ... fertility and drouth ... the sowing and the harvest ... hard work ... loneliness ... freezing grey dawns ... evenings around the fire ... the simple pleasures ... and always the struggle for existence."

Ellis wove in contemporary topics of rural farm life via a "Culture Club" that met periodically in the storyline, allowing her to smoothly insert pitches for products for Sears-Roebuck, the potential sponsor. In fact, more than her other two serial ideas, *Wide Horizons* served as an expanded variation of her *Travels of Mary Ward* program, directly referencing items found in current Sears catalogs via page, price, and even payment plan options.

John McMillan and his wife Anne were the core around which all the storylines and pathos were expected to revolve. John, or Mac, a hardworking farmer, was "a real man of the soil ... but with education" and a "streak of poetry in him." Anne, however, represented his cultural opposite, a "charming, gay ... witty" New Yorker who was nevertheless a salt-of-the-earth wife for John, a "real farmer's helpmate" determined to make their house a home.

Additional characters created for the serial were Jean Warren, a friend of Anne's and former heiress devastated by the loss of her family's fortune, and Jean's father Stanley Warren, "a broken old man" having lost all his property. The town of Elk's Landing was populated by the likes of Howard and Belle Jones ("up to date" with a "swell sense of humor") and their children, Fritzie Jones and her "radical ideas," Ellie Barnes the town busybody, Doc Beavins the town pharmacist and confidant to all, Cousin Hattie the up-to-date business proprietor, and Zeb, a "Will Rogers-y . . . homespun philosopher."

Creating tension in the show were Bess Crawford, John's former sweetheart who has now made a pact with Guy Travers – the man who pried away the Warren's fortune – to destroy the McMillans' lives. To the McMillans' chagrin, Travers' dirty work was done under the table and hidden by legal maneuvers, making him an honest beacon of success to the rest of the community.

Ultimately, *River to the Sea*, *The Marsh Family*, and *Wide Horizons* never made it commercially to the air. By the 1940s the soap opera market was fully developed and very profitable. Dominated by the likes of Frank and Anne Hummert, Irna Phillips, and Elaine Carrington, it was all but impossible for an outsider like Caroline Ellis who lacked the connections in Chicago radio to get a second chance. Now in her 60s, it's unlikely Ellis had the desire, energy, and drive to return to Chicago, still one of the most competitive radio markets in the country, and try to establish herself against well-entrenched creators who had years of success and multiple credits to their names. It also would have required additional outlay by Arthur Church for Ellis' living expenses in Chicago without the income *Golden Store* had generated earlier. With KMBC's eight-man band the Texas Rangers relocated to Southern California and struggling to find regular performing and broadcasting income, Church was surely reluctant to commit yet more money to such out-of-state ventures.

Part 4: Back in Kansas City

The Happy Home

In 1941 Ellis set aside her creative burst of new serial drama programs and began preparing a new show to pitch to national advertisers. Arthur Church guaranteed a fifteen-minute time slot Monday through Saturday for Ellis to work out her new premise entitled *The Happy Home*. In a turn from the formula that had proven successful for much of her radio work, Ellis planned to do away with storylines and dramatic action and talk directly to her devoted listeners; in essence, to air a much more standard women's homemaker show. The program was billed as "a quarter-hour of conversation – some news, some philosophy" and commentary on areas of interest to her female audience. Ellis was not adverse to interviewing guests or reading from a short story that caught her eye.

Fran Heyser's return to Kansas City was delayed an extra two years and he did not return permanently until 1942. After spending the two years in Des Moines and Chicago with Ellis on *Caroline's Golden Store*, he had been sent by Church to Hollywood where he supervised the recording of a transcription library for the Texas Rangers, KMBC's headlining Western musical act that had relocated to California in 1939. Upon landing back in Kansas City he reunited with Ellis on *The Happy Home*.

With the United States at war in the early 1940s, homemaking broadcasts such as that developed by Ellis were more pertinent than ever. While she strove to be "inspirational," "thought-provoking," and "entertaining," Ellis knew that the essence of her success was her relevance to the housewives of middle-America. Tips to extend the life of household appliances and tools and strategies to conserve energy and fuel were important to women who were both on tight budgets and wanting to do their patriotic duty in conserving materials and resources for the war effort. Her contributions to that effort via daily broadcasts were recognized on January 6, 1943, when it was announced that KMBC had received a *Variety* Show

Management Award for its broadcasting work in support of the armed forces. The station specifically singled Ellis out as an important contributor to winning the honor.

During the early years of *The Happy Home* between 1941 and 1944, Caroline Ellis achieved significant ratings milestones. For a time she pulled in larger audiences in the Kansas City market than *The Story of Mary Marlin*, a Chicago-originated nationwide daily serial about an Iowa housewife who becomes a United States Senator. Marlin kept her audience coming back every day for eighteen years. More impressive than this ratings coup was a period during which Ellis was scheduled against sudsy queen *Ma Perkins*. Played by Virginia Payne for 27 years from 1933 to 1960, *Ma Perkins* was a perennial favorite for female audiences; Ellis again came out on top in the Kansas City ratings. The city's listeners clearly loved their hometown homemaker. Eventually *The Happy Home* was moved to an 8:30 a.m. spot, before the soap operas began to air in the later morning. In that slot Ellis received an impressive 28% audience share, 10% higher than her closest competitor.

Despite such impressive numbers, Arthur B. Church's sales staff was never able to find a coast-to-coast or even Midwestern regional sponsor for Caroline Ellis' tips and hints program. In an attempt to appeal to a wider array of potential advertisers, various sponsorship rates were put in place in the mid-1940s. Once-a-week sponsorship cost 83$ per week for the quarter-hour broadcast, 48$ for time and 35$ for talent. A three-a-week plan cost $234.60, $129.60 for time and $105 for talent. Note that there was no discount for more frequent sponsoring. Interestingly, *The Happy Home* apparently was not available for daily sponsorship; either the sales team for some reason thought there wouldn't be any interest in a six-per-week series as there had been just a few years earlier, or Ellis no longer aired six times a week on that program as she did when *The Happy Home* first went on the air. As a further enticement to potential buyers, Church even allowed the salesmen to guarantee that the program would be safe from any network time encroachment.

In 1942 KMBC was awarded a Management Citation by *Variety* magazine for its work toward the war effort. Ellis' work was singled out for "combatting anti-United Nations propaganda and race prejudice. Her good intentions weren't always so well rewarded. Ellis briefly initiated a program entitled *Letters to Soldiers* in which she matched up members of the armed services with listeners who would like to act as pen pals. Some of the soldiers, however, reveled in the opportunity to write to girls back home and their racy letters caused a backlash, prompting KMBC to scrap the effort.

Via *The Happy Home* Ellis created a unique connection with her listeners day in and day out. The daily quarter hour was ostensibly just another homemaker show, a genre that had been a staple of the airwaves practically from the medium's inception. But Ellis, widowed for two decades by this time and a woman who had worked regularly since that time, was anything but the typical housewife these types of programs sought to personify. A review of some surviving scripts from this era provide insight to the wide range of topics she touched upon, from the best ways to clean dishes to political events in faraway nations.

The earliest surviving script from the series, dated March 17, 1941, hints at the audience to which Ellis was attempting appeal; a growing and urbanizing segment of women in bustling Kansas City

Caroline broadcasts with a women's group. Courtesy Steve Crockett.

mixed with rural Kansas and Missouri women who still toiled from sunup to sundown on the region's farms. Caroline Ellis recounted her earlier years on the farm:

> But first, when the butchering was done and the lard rendered, there were the crackling and the skins left. Of course the best of the cracklings went into that food for the gods, --crackling corn bread. Man – man! A hunk of crackling corn bread and a glass of milk on a cold winter day! Umph! But we do get enough, in time, of anything – even food for the gods. So the rest of the cracklings and the fried out skins would go into the old washboiler set in the cellar for that purpose. And then would be added all winter long, bacon rinds, ham parings, bits of fat, all meat waste of every kind.

By phrasing this description in the past tense it recalled memories for Kansas City's urbanites who grew up on turn-of-the-century farms or fondly remembered the farms of their parents or grandparents. At the same time her monolog was instantly recognizable to rural listeners who were more than familiar with the process of making everyday corn bread – food of the gods, no less! – and saving the skin of the slaughtered pigs for cracklings. Ellis continued on that same program:

> Mrs. Farmer would say to Mr. Farmer – "John, if you'll get the kettle out in the yard for me this morning, I believe I'll make soap today and get it done with. Housecleaning'll be along before we know it." So the big iron kettle was ragged out by the wood pile, where fuel would be handy, and set up on some flat stones, level and solid and a fired kindled under it. I wonder how many people have ever known the joy of building a fire out in the open.

Whether her audience had ever, in fact, started such a fire outdoors, it was an event listeners could be proud of having done while smiling knowingly at the joy it did, in fact, bring or picturing romantically in their minds if they had not ever done so. With a nod to her years as a dramatic writer, Ellis eloquently described the tedious, mundane act of starting the fire:

All the suspense and then the waiting – that tiny first blaze, smelling of burning leaves and dry chips wavering, almost dying, while you watch breathlessly and blow gently – kneeling down in the dirt – feeding it with little slivers of pine and bits of bark – then finally with real wood as the smoke rolls up and the flame roars under the kettle and your fire is going at last.

A year later in 1942, with the United States fully committed to fighting the Axis Powers abroad, Caroline Ellis didn't hesitate to discuss the war's events with her homebound listeners. Where were these strange-sounding places her listeners heard about on daily war bulletins and newscasts? She attempted to address just that issue in her broadcast from September 17, 1942. German Field Marshal Erwin Rommel had attempted earlier that summer to drive into Egypt from the west toward Alexandria, Cairo, and the Suez Canal. Stalled in their effort by Commonwealth forces at the First Battle of El Alamein, the Germans initiated a new offensive, known as the Battle of Alam el Halfa, that lasted from August 30 to September 5 but also failed to break through Commonwealth defenses.

With the combat in northern Egypt prominent in the news in print and on the air, Ellis decided to "go out after a little knowledge" and enlighten her listeners about a distant place called Suez. She intoned that she "believe[d] we will find it interesting to look for a few minutes at what this canal is and how it got that way and what gives it all this importance." Ellis began with its geographic location between Africa and the Arabian Desert of Asia and implored her audience to get a map handy to better understand events there.

Ellis briefly and simply outlined the economic importance of the Suez Canal to British commerce, and the tremendous distance it abbreviated for shipping lines to India. Along the way she highlighted the trek of British vessels past Italy through the Mediterranean Sea toward the Suez, thus accounting for the naval fighting listeners heard about in that region. She provided background for Kansas City's homemakers, tracing the history of the idea for a Suez Canal back to 1300 BC and projects during the reigns of Seti the First, Rameses the Great, and Darius I. Ellis' history lesson

Promotional picture of Caroline reading fan mail. Courtesy Steve Crockett.

jumped to more modern history and the perseverance of French engineer Ferdinand de Lesseps in getting the Suez Canal initiated.

This historical exploration led to details of de Lesseps' life, including his relationship with Sa'id Ali and a brief look at world events in 1859, the year construction began on the canal. Ellis described the grand festivities around the Canal's opening ten years later: "The great assembly feasted and drank and all was friendship and love – on the surface – no matter what daggers were hidden in what sleeves . . . Well, in a few days all the rulers and the royalty went back home to get busy with their wars again. They'd had a nice holiday, and the great ditch was left there, shining in the sun." But it was England's prime minister, Benjamin Disraeli, Ellis pointed out who recognized the potential of the "ditch," and convinced his government to pay nearly four million pounds to Egypt in return for controlling shares in the Suez.

Why spend so much time on the dry and rather arcane history of the Suez that seemed secondary to its value to the Axis and Allied combatants? Primarily because Ellis found the topic interesting; in fact, she preempted any listener complaints about the topic by simply claiming "I hope you were interested in what I have been saying. For myself, I like to know the why of things . . . And if anybody would like a copy of this condensed history of Suez, I'll be glad to send it." What listener would dare admit she didn't have a curiosity and interest in the greater world, the "why" of world-changing events? In fact, they may even have been proud of making it through Ellis' quarter-hour review of the 110-year-old waterway.

Two-and-one-half years later Ellis struck a very different tone on April 13, 1945, when she reflected on the sudden death of President Franklin D. Roosevelt. Her broadcast began like so many that day, recognizing his leadership in a world in the flames of World War II. Roosevelt was "the captain on whom we relied to guide us through those rocks we know loom ahead, in the coming reorganization of the family of nations of the world." But Ellis went beyond sweeping eulogies for the heralded president, a man beloved by many but yet unknown at any personal level by *The Happy Home*'s listenership.

She briefly encouraged "kindly thoughts" and prayers on the man who had to take up Roosevelt's mantle, who now had to carry the great burden. But Ellis' focus quickly honed in on the person who was most likely to strike a sympathetic chord with her audience and attract their sympathy: Roosevelt's widow, Eleanor.

> And as women, today our thoughts and sympathy are with Mrs. Eleanor Roosevelt. Sorrow strikes alike in mansion and in cottage. Sorrow is no respecter of persons nor of circumstances. Today, Eleanor Roosevelt is not a president's wife, nor an international figure. Today, Eleanor Roosevelt

is just a stricken woman, mourning for her husband, even as you and I.

In a few short sentences Ellis brought Roosevelt down to a personal level, a woman to whom homemakers, farmers' wives, and working women alike could relate. Ellis created a space where Roosevelt's pedigree wasn't important and where her controversial political stances could be set aside. For these moments the President's wife was one of them:

> She has means, and she has her children. But money – children – nor any honor nor acclaim the world can give, ever takes the place of the man we married in the springtime of our youth – planned life together, and expected to sit down together when the evening shadows descended. "Grow old with me – the best is yet to be – the last of life for which the first was made."

Was Caroline Ellis thinking of her own marriage as she spoke into the microphone? Was she sharing the expectations she had as a younger woman before she lost her husband, Charles, so early? Ellis continued, "We can almost hear him say – 'Go on with your living, you folks. Don't worry about me. I'm all right.'" Perhaps such words had provided her comfort through the years and she hoped they would be that comfort to her audience as well.

On August 15, 1945, Ellis savored the peace that had come to the Earth with Japan's surrender just hours before (also August 15 in Japan). Her words reflected the relief of so many around the world:

> Well, friends, it has come – the day when we can say: "It's all over." Perhaps not literally, but in intent, wa[r] has ceased. There is no war in all the world today! Let's say that over again – and slowly, so as to savor it as fully as it's possible for us to. The world is free today – free of war. In all the world there is no war – not in Europe – nor in Asia – not in England – not in Greece – nor in the Near East – nor on any of the seven sea[s]. Someway it makes it more real to name the places.

Caroline Ellis talks with Boy Scouts. Courtesy Steve Crockett.

A year before, in May 1944 the decision was made to go to a six-per-week schedule and *The Happy Home* added a second sponsor, Three-Flavor Red Heart Dog Food. To promote this new pet product on Tuesdays, Thursdays, and Saturdays, the dog food producer offered bright red plastic identification lockets that could be snapped on to dog collars as well as dog training booklets. The series continued under the sponsorship of the John J. Jelke Company's Good Luck Margarine on Mondays, Wednesdays, and Fridays. In August 1944 Mentholatum took sponsoring responsibilities for the Tuesday and Thursday broadcasts. Other sponsors during the next several years included the Celanese Corporation of America and Hollanderizin Corporation (1945), the Celanese Corporation and Marshall Hatcheries, Marshall, MO (1949), the Drackett Company, makers of Drano and Windex (1950), and the Celanese Corporation and Gland-O-Lac Co (1951).

David Andrews. Courtesy Steve Crockett.

David Andrews

As early as 1948 David Andrews, who also emceed KMBC's breakfast show *Rhymaline Time*, was appearing regularly on *The Happy Home* and was even identified in station materials as Ellis' "dialog partner." Born George Cirotto on September 28, 1921, David Andrews grew up in New York City and attended Haaren High School (since closed) where he earned roles in the school's plays and musicals. His parents and two older brothers also had musical backgrounds. After graduating Andrews got a job with the Postal Telegraph Company but grew tired of the work and decided to join the Civilian Conservation Corps, much to his parents' dismay. He spent his service time in Boville, ID, before returning to New York and getting a job with the Platt-Forbes Advertising Agency. After eighteen months Andrews enlisted in the Army Air Corps but wound up in an infantry unit training at Ft. Jackson, SC. He volunteered for the gas warfare school but a mishap in a gas-recognition chamber resulted in a hospital stay with complications from pneumonia.

Andrews' outfit was shipped to Salina, KS, where he joined them after more than a month in the hospital. In Salina he received a disability discharge and met a local girl, Loretta Beck, whom he courted and then married in 1942. A local company, H. D. Lee Co., had an opening in its advertising department that was perfect for Andrews and he went to work on both their radio and newspaper ad campaigns. After meeting with the general manager of station KSAL to buy some time, Andrews ended up accepting a new position with the radio station. Eventually he began considering a return to New York and in 1944 arranged to meet a Platt-Forbes Agency executive in Kansas City to discuss some options.

After driving in to Kansas City from Salina, Andrews was persuaded to audition with KMBC. Program manager Rod Cupp immediately hired Andrews before New York could snatch him back. Rather than working in sales he was put to work performing in various capacities including announcer, emcee and writer of *Rhymaline Time*, emcee and singer on *Brush Creek Follies*, assistant on Ellis' *The Happy Home*, and actor on *American Story*, "Magic Book," *Of Health and Happiness*, and *The Joanne Taylor Show*.

Bea Johnson and her Successors

After a decade writing and hosting *The Happy Home*, the bulk of the program was turned over to Bea Johnson for the 1952-1953 season. Johnson, who had worked at KMBC as far back as 1936, soon turned *The Happy Home* into a full half-hour show. A seasoned and talented homemaker broadcast professional in her own right, Johnson comes across in the historical record as playing second fiddle to Ellis as this was the second time she took over a show Ellis had created and nurtured into local popularity. Johnson had also taken Ellis' place on *Joanne Taylor Fashion Flashes* in 1936 when Caroline Ellis left to produce *The Travels of Mary Ward*. That she was a lesser Caroline Ellis couldn't be further from the truth. In fact, it was during Johnson's time helming *Joanne Taylor* that the show received a commendation from *Billboard* for having the highest listener ratings of any female broadcaster, a first-place award from the same publication for Midwestern daytime programs, and an Award of Merit from the National Retail Dry Goods Association (NRDGA).

A graduate of the University of Missouri's School of Journalism, Johnson helmed *Joanne Taylor* for five years until 1941 when she took a hiatus from radio upon the birth of her daughter. Rather than quit working altogether Johnson debuted a fashion and beauty column entitled "Especially For You" that was picked up by a number of regional newspapers. At the end of World War II Bea Johnson gave birth to a second daughter and subsequently shifted her literary focus to freelance projects at the expense of her column. Finding only middling success in that endeavor, beginning in 1946 Johnson went to work for an agency as a special script writer. She was active with the Gamma Alpha Chi, a national honorary advertising sorority that has since merged with Alpha Delta Sigma, and served as president on two occasions, 1944 – 1948 and 1952 – 1954. She also served as National Expansion Director for a period of time.

Johnson would return briefly to KMBC in 1949 to take over as hostess of another domestic program, *Happy Kitchen*, while management sought out a replacement. In 1941 Nancy Goode had been given the job based on her strong credentials working as a home service advisor for Kansas Gas & Electric Co. in Wichita. She left in 1945 to get married and was subsequently replaced by Winnifred Cannon. Cannon had earned her B.S. in home economics and journalism from Iowa State University and before being hired by the station worked for the Department of Agriculture, Swift and Company, and most recently the American Meat Institute in Chicago. On air she was known as "Betty Parker" and a 1949 mail survey supported the show's results: Listener mail was received from over 150 counties across six states. Cannon, who had a long career as a home economist outside of radio under her married name Winnifred Cannon Jardine, was replaced by Bea Johnson just long enough for KMBC to find a suitable replacement in Myrtle Wiley.

On January 16, 1950 Wiley assumed the helm of *Happy Kitchen* to the excitement of station brass, who felt her to be the strongest hostess since Beulah Kearney and Kay Neuman. A new co-sponsorship model, allowing multiple advertisers to buy time on the show intrigued them as well. KMBC and sister Midland Broadcasting Company station KFRM laid out strict word counts for advertisers to include in each of the program's scripts. Multiple memos and conversations flew back and forth among top executives hashing out the exact count; one pushed for 175 words for full participants (advertisers sponsoring all six of the *Happy Kitchen*'s weekly shows) while another thought 75 words was acceptable and in line with the stations' pricing practices. In addition to on-air plugs, executives made sure the sponsors were highlighted in other *Happy Kitchen* publicity efforts including newspaper ads, displays at the Kansas City Electric Association Show and the Kansas and Missouri State Fairs, and quarterly mailings to grocers in the Kansas City metropolitan area.

As part of their *Happy Kitchen* promotional efforts, KMBC-KFRM renewed their contract with Kansas City Power & Light Company (KCP&L) to lease a modern, fully electric demonstration and exhibition kitchen the company had in a downtown office building. Once a week the *Happy Kitchen* hostess would lead a cooking demonstration in the space utilizing various sponsor products for a live audience. The presentation, which often took an hour or more, was subsequently edited down to thirty minutes for broadcast during a Saturday morning (9:15 – 9:45) slot. In negotiating this additional job duty Wiley had a new electric range installed at her personal apartment at the station's expense in order for her to properly prepare for the recorded demonstrations.

Radio Schoolhouse and "The Magic Book"

While broadcasting her daily women's show *The Happy Home* remained Caroline Ellis' primary responsibility during the 1940s, she was also assigned other broadcasting responsibilities by Arthur Church. Perhaps no others were as well-received in the Kansas City area as the children's production called "The Magic Book." The non-commercial series featured new stories and retellings of classic tales geared toward a preschool and early elementary listening audience. This once-per-week feature was part of KMBC's daily *Radio Schoolhouse*.

KMBC Schoolhouse premiered October 9, 1944, as a three times weekly program. As would be its format over a decade-long run, each day of the week had a unique theme. Monday's program was called "Inside the News" and hosted by Erle Smith, the head of the KMBC's news department. Smith supplemented his review of the week's events with a guest report from a student newscaster with news from local schools. Wednesday's "Fun With Facts" featured a different class being quizzed in history and science by *KMBC Schoolhouse* "principal" R. Edwin Browne, educational director of the station. Friday's "The Magic Book," was written by Caroline Ellis who dubbed herself the Keeper of the Magic Book. During the show's initial season Ellis dramatized stories from the supplementary reading lists of the area schools. Some of the earliest stories chosen for reenactment by Ellis were "Little Golden Hood" (December 1, 1944), "The Grateful Beasts" (December 8, 1944), "Goose Girl" (December 15, 1944), "Cinderella and the Glass Slipper" (December 22, 1944), and "Puss-in-Boots" (December 29, 1944). The series aired from 3:00 to 3:15, immediately following *CBS American School of the Air*.

Due to the popularity of *KMBC Schoolhouse*, the station increased its frequency on the airwaves during the 1945-1946 season. Ellis' "The Magic Book" was moved to Tuesdays while her old Friday time spot was filled with "Curtain Call," a series of dramatic sketches performed by Kansas City-area high school students. Participants were chosen from The All City High School Radio Workshop, itself a competitive program that pulled from promising students among the city's high school speech classes. A new Thursday feature, "Music Time," filled out the weekly slate of broadcasts. The daily educational show matched up well with its commercial competition. Surveys said "Music Time" was the most popular installment overall, attracting

30.8% of listeners compared to 19.2% for the 2nd place show. "Curtain Call" did very well also, with 29.1% of radio listeners tuning in, comparable to its highest rated competition. "Inside the News" and "Fun With Facts" claimed 28% and 26.9% of listeners respectively, beating the other afternoon serials. Only Ellis' "The Magic Book" failed to win its timeslot, earning 22.2% of the radio audience compared to 29.7% for the top-rated show. KMBC kept the program geared toward the youngest listeners, insisting that its limited appeal to older listeners didn't diminish its overall value.

Writing for an audience as young as that intended for "The Magic Book" provided unique challenges for Ellis as she explained in an address at Omaha's Creighton University at a District Meeting for the Association of Women Radio Directors. While deciding with an advisory group of teachers that fairy tales were the best choice for a source of material for the show, actually selecting and adapting the tales proved to be exceedingly difficult at times. Many of the beloved children's stories were quite long, too long to be effectively trimmed to a fifteen-minute script. Even more, the content of many was objectionable by broadcasting standards:

> There is likely no more tragic and cruel writing in our language than the old fairy tales – as they are. It may be one thing to read to a child about torture and killing and gouging out of eyes and boiling in oil and cracking of bones but it is quite another thing to put such material on the air in dramatic form, with sound effects.

From the premier of "The Magic Book" Ellis laid out criteria by which each episode would abide. First, she eliminated every hint of cruelty a story might contain. Not even bad manners or disrespect toward elders would find a place in her scripts. Any instances of such behavior had to be punished in some way during the course of the story, and the punishment had to be a natural outcome of circumstances, not meted out intentionally by a character. Any sort of derogatory description was edited. She noted, for instance, that "hunchbacks" were referred to as dwarfs and gnomes and "old crones" or "cruel stepmothers" were changed to witches. After all, just because a woman was a stepmother did not automatically mean she was cruel. Further, "a man isn't mean and parsimonious and dishonest, just because he is a rich man," so wealthy men were transformed into "old misers" when necessary. When possible, Ellis made sure over the course of a story that any evil characters "repent and become good folks," escaping punishment they may rightfully have deserved. She also insisted on formal language with proper grammar and diction. While such attitudes toward story writing had contributed to many of the General Mills complaints against her *Caroline's Golden Store* program years before, they seemed more suited to the fare she now found herself writing.

What it lacked in revenue for KMBC, "The Magic Book" made up for with critical recognition received during its run. In 1946 the series received a First Award from the Institute for Education by Radio at Ohio State University. The citation, awarded "in the regional station classification for school broadcasts, primary grades," singled out "The Magic Book" for its "outstanding educational value and distinguished radio production." Further, the judges lauded the program "for the preparation of a delightful story hour which entertains and stimulates the imagination of kindergarten and primary grade children. The program helps its young listeners to acquire a better vocabulary and an appreciation of good reading." For the award application process KMBC submitted Ellis' script "Blackie Takes a Trip," about a small black cat that wandered into the strange world of china cats, as representative of the series.

These accolades earned by "The Magic Book" were feathers in the cap for Arthur Church and KMBC, which had racked up two other notable awards in the two prior months of 1946. First, *Variety* recognized KMBC with its *Variety* Show Management Award for knowing best "How to Run a Radio Station" and then the City College of New York singled out KMBC as "The Most Effective All-Over Station Promotion by a Regional Radio Station."

In 1947 *KMBC Schoolhouse*, since renamed *Radio Schoolhouse*, was added to KMBC's sister station KFRM, a farm-oriented station originating from separate studios in Kansas. The station reached far into rural Kansas and into sections of Nebraska, Oklahoma, and even Colorado. Its five weekly broadcasts continued to each boast a unique theme: Monday's feature, "Tomorrow's Farmer" was new to the line-up and was geared toward high school classes in agriculture, economics, and the social sciences. "Fun With Facts," now moved to Tuesdays, was curated by a new host, Lee Stewart. Ellis' "The Magic Book" was bumped to Wednesdays and "Music Time" which featured Alice Gallup, at the time the supervisor of Kansas City's music education program, presenting musical lessons for elementary students, remained on Thursdays. "Youth Views the News," now with a youth panel in addition to KMBC-KFRM news editor Erle Smith, wrapped up the week as the Friday broadcast.

The Radio Schoolhouse line-up continued to be modified over the years, though many of the daily installments remained familiar. During the 1952-1953 season, nearly ten years after its debut, three of the five daily series within the *Schoolhouse* week schedule had been around for many years. Tuesday's installment was still entitled "Fun With Facts" but the focus had changed to a science-themed broadcast for elementary students. Ellis' "The Magic Book" on Thursdays and "Music Time" on Fridays were holdovers from the first and second seasons respectively. "Music Time" eventually began challenging "The Magic Book" in earning broadcast awards, receiving back-to-back First Awards from Ohio State University in 1947 and 1948. New offerings in 1953 included Monday's show, "The Art Lesson," an aural presentation of a class completing an art project, and Wednesday's "Youth Looks Ahead," presentations for high school students exploring vocational options with professionals and a faculty moderator.

Variety review from April 2, 1947.

> KMBC Schoolhouse of the Air
> With Caroline Ellis, Eric Smith, Keith Payton, others
> Director: Dr. Charles F. Church
> Producer: Fran Heiser [sic]
> Sustaining
> 30 Mins.; Tues., Thurs., 2 p.m.
> KMBC, Kansas City
>
> The afternoon listening audience of schoolkids built up by CBS's "School of the Air" on Mondays, Wednesdays and Fridays is too good a setup to ignore on other days of the

week, according to the education department at KMBC. Accordingly, the station calls up some of its top talent to put on a couple of half-hours weekly to keep the school audience at the listening post right across the board at 2 p.m. weekdays.

The two stanzas actually are made up of four regular quarter-hours. "The Magic Book" and "Fun With Facts" on Tuesdays and "Inside the News" and "Music Time" on Thursdays. The "Magic Book" period is the work of Caroline Ellis, a well-established radio veteran in this area, who offers the schoolkids dramatic versions of fairy tales and other literary favorites. Her session is combined with the "Fun With Facts" period, a class recitation format for the upper grades, on Tuesdays.

Eric Smith, the station's news chief, shares a Thursday quarter hour with a guest student newscaster. Smith offers a review of the week's news in his standard style, while the guester comes through with news in and about the schools. This is completed with a session with music, usually held in an actual schoolroom and transcribed. This one had the kiddies singing under Miss Alice Gallup, music teacher.

The two half-hours add up to thoughtful programming in an effort to dovetail with the American School of the Air broadcasts. While the programs class as civic service, they are also effective local promotion, for they have the local name appeal for listeners not present in the net shows.

The combination gives the school crowd good listening daily at 2 p.m.

Radio-based education never matched the ambitions envisioned by early radio pioneers in the 1920s, but this particular effort – though very local – must be considered a success. Survey results of the 1952 – 1953 season indicated a minimum regular listenership of 3,866 classrooms and over 110,000 students each week. Interestingly, Caroline Ellis' "The Magic Book" claimed the highest audience at nearly 32,000 student listeners in a given week, even though it was regularly one of the poorest performing segments for wider audiences according to the Hooper ratings. Friday's "Music Time" reached nearly 29,000 students and Monday's "The Art Lesson" nearly 27,000. The vocational feature on Wednesday, "Youth Looks Ahead," only managed 5,000 student listeners a week.

KMBC Radio Institute

Trained to be a school teacher before he was lured into the radio industry in the 19-teens, throughout his lifetime Arthur Church continued to value education and was not reluctant to devote station resources to educational programming. When trying to sell original programming to sponsors, Church and his staff frequently promoted the educational aspects of the show under consideration.

One of Church's proudest moments in the field of educational radio was the debut of KMBC's first Radio Institute for Teachers, a three-week production that ran from June 11 – 29, 1945, at Kansas City Junior College. Under the direction of the station's head of education Dr. Charles F. Church, KMBC teamed up with the Kansas City Public School System and the University of Kansas to produce the Institute. The event brought numerous radio professionals – many from the affiliated CBS network – to Kansas City along with three hundred teachers from around the region. Through the university's School of Education and Graduate School, participants could even get two hours of college credit for participating at a cost of $8.

The Institute was a natural fit for Caroline Ellis, a former teacher herself and one of the KMBC staff members most involved in KMBC's weekly *Radio Schoolhouse* productions. Among her activities with the Radio Institute for Teachers were leading a symposium on "Public Service in Radio," leading a reenactment of one of her scripts, "The Little Rabbit That Wanted Red Wings" from "The Magic Book," and participating in panels on "News in Radio" and "Philosophy of Radio."

One of the headlining presenters was Dr. Lyman Bryson, who had received the "Four Bomb" citation from the Writers' War Board and spoke on the differences between using radio and other mediums as a sales vehicle. Other participants included Bill Downs, a war correspondent for CBS and former Kansas City journalist who spoke on "News in Radio" and "Radio in Wartime," Mortimer Frankel, an associate script editor from CBS who led some scriptwriting sessions, and C.E. Hooper, president of the widely used C.E. Hooper, Inc. ratings agency, who talked about "Research and Evaluation" in the radio field.

Ellis wasn't the only KMBC staff member to participate in the Institute. KMBC's technical director, Robin D. Compton, gave a presentation on radio equipment for school use, while Karl Koerper, managing director, Kenneth Krahl, studio supervisor, Sam Molen, sports director, Sam Bennett, head of sales, and Ray Moler, chief Engineer, all had roles during the course of the event. Whatever success both in critical and financial terms the Institute experienced it wasn't enough for Church to repeat in following years.

One Minute Dramas

There are rare pieces of evidence that Caroline Ellis occasionally proposed or was asked to pitch a new series for KMBC. One such idea presented to Arthur Church Productions was called *One Minute Dramas*. Each episode – only one minute in length – centered on a single page from an advertiser's sales catalog. A script sample chose p. 659 in the Sears catalog which featured "wool yard goods." It quickly opens with a woman complaining about her inability to determine if some sample wool is good enough to create items that won't wear out too soon. Ellis is right there to offer reassuring advice: "For your coat, turn to page 659. Materials on page 659 are such as you will find in coats up to $39.95 – in many stores. I suggest you consider the worsted boucle, since there is no lovelier coating material, nor one which stays in style better."

In another spec script, "Power Washer – Page 940," Ellis restores some marital peace between John and Mary. Mary, so busy taking care of the home, asks her husband if they "couldn't possibly afford a power washer." Hearing a sympathetic "no" from her husband, worn out Mary goes to bed. Luckily, Ellis is there to offer sage advice to John. "Get your Sears' catalogue and do a little reading," she directs him, "Turn to page 940. And read Sears' generous offer to place a power washer in your home, for thirty days, without one cent of cost to you, so that you may see for yourself how the drudgery of wash day may all be done away with." Before he can protest about cost she assures John: "It may be purchased on Sears' easy payment plan, making the payments monthly."

End of a Career

Caroline Ellis' *The Happy Home* may have started as a short-term project to keep Ellis busy while she, Church, and KMBC's executives decided how best to utilize their star female broadcaster. However, it turned out to be her most long-running series for the station. A native Kansan herself, Ellis' voice remained fairly unknown for much of her career to listeners outside the eastern portion of the state due to KMBC's broadcast pattern that was much stronger to Iowa and Missouri to the east. In 1947, the same year Ellis celebrated her 70th birthday, the Midland Broadcasting Company built a new transmitter in north-central Kansas to which KMBC's broadcasts were transmitted and then aired to much of Kansas. While a step down from her year-long run on NBC-Red's

Caroline Ellis interviews in the field. Courtesy Steve Crockett.

Midwest circuit with *Caroline's Golden Store*, the remaining years of her career were nonetheless impressive with a listenership from Eastern Colorado to the Mississippi River.

By 1952 the 75-year-old Ellis began to slow down and, as mentioned above, relinquished the microphone of *The Happy Home* for the Monday through Friday broadcasts to Bea Johnson. The following review from the October 22, 1952 issue of *Variety* revealed the industry magazine's take on the shakeup.

> The Happy Home
> With Bea Johnson, David Andrews
> Producer: Fran Heyser
> Writer: Mrs. Johnson
> 30 Mins., 8:30 a.m. Mon.-Fri.
> Participating
> KMBC-KFRM, Kansas City
>
> Morning half-hour for femme listeners recently has been taken over by Bea Johnson in a major program shift by KMBC and its outstate Kansas affiliate, KFRM. Two former quarter hours, "The Happy Home" and "The Happy Kitchen," are now combined in this one segment in which Mrs. Johnson covers the full range of women's topics. She covers fashions, household hints, cookery, child care, women in the news, etc. with David Andrews of the station staff along as sidekick, commentator and recipe writer.
>
> It's a return to the air for Mrs. Johnson who served the station in the late 1930s as "Joanne Taylor," an established program for the John Taylor department store. In the interim she has done agency work, lecturing, writing and raised two daughters. Generally prominent on the local and area scene, she is a fitting candidate for heading up the station's department of women's interests.
>
> As the program is working out it evidently is imminently satisfactory to the station and to the listeners. It generally carries its full quota of spots, most of them on a semi-permanent basis, and in that light is profitable to the station.

Listener-wise the show comes off satisfactorily, as Mrs. Johnson gives it something of a personality touch and leaves no doubt that she has been around in the world of homemaking, public contacts and better living. She takes the straightforward approach in most of her airings, with Andrews ad libbing and giving the show a lighter cast. As broadcast it evidently relies 100% on script, and possibly suffers somewhat at times being a bit stiff. It could stand a bit of casualness in the doing.

Saturday "Happy Home" is handled by Caroline Ellis, who for many years handled it daily in a quarter-hour morning segment. One of KMBC's alltime radio favorites, and one with national recognition, Mrs. Ellis picks up the weekend show where Mrs. Johnson leaves off and maintains the interest level nicely. New set up represents something of an easing off in the work load for her, much deserved after more than a score of years on the air.

The last extant scripts for Ellis' show are dated from the early months of 1953. So, while the written record doesn't point to the exact date that Caroline Ellis finally decided to step away from the microphone, evidence suggests it was 1953, very possibly after the 1952-1953 season. Arthur B. Church, who started selling amateur radio parts forty years earlier, also began planning the sale of KMBC and the Midland Broadcasting Company that year. In light of Ellis' long admiration for Church it is very likely that the thought of adjusting to a new owner and boss was highly unappealing and, combined with her age, the last straw that induced her to leave the industry for good.

Church finalized the plans for the sale in 1954 when Kansas City's Cook Paint and Varnish Company, which had owned the cross-town Mutual-affiliated rival WHB since 1930, took ownership. Television was likely the driving force behind the deal; Cook sold WHB's radio division but kept the television division which they subsequently combined with KMBC's television organization, a technological area that Church had been studying and directing resources toward since the 1930s. Without a daily program of

Bea Johnson's Happy Home Cookbook. From author's collection.

her own anymore and probably seeing no future for herself in the emerging visual field, Ellis was able to gracefully exit on her own terms before being pushed out.

After retiring from KMBC Ellis went to work for a short time for insurance provider Blue Cross. There's no record of what she actually did for the company and even her great-nephew 65 years later suspected Ellis may have owed her position more to her friendship with one of the company's national directors than due to any specific skill set she had honed. In her final years Ellis moved around staying with different family members rather than settling down in her own home. Ellis' family recalled their impressions that she never seemed completely satisfied during her post-broadcasting years before she died on May 17, 1963, in Richland, Shawnee Co. KS. Memorial services were held at the Evangelical United Brethren Church in Richland and she is buried at the Richland Cemetery in rural Shawnee, KS.

Legacy

Assessing Caroline's Ellis broadcasting legacy is complicated at best. It's interesting to consider there would likely be no discussion in the first place if she hadn't decided to leave Detroit in 1928. She had a growing career in the department store sector that surely would have continued unabated as demonstrated by the immediate years after her return to Kansas City. Her introduction to broadcasting was a complete fluke brought about only by her friendship with Burris Jenkins. While Detroit certainly had its own thriving radio market, there's no evidence that suggests she might have happened into a connection with radio producers or advertisers as happened in Kansas City.

One might argue that Ellis tried to push herself too soon and too quickly into new genres of radio where she had little experience and where the competition was highly developed and cutthroat. Her time writing *Caroline's Golden Store* allowed Ellis to mash her tried-and-true sales-pitch-infused stories with the melodrama of popular soap operas. It seems, however, that Caroline took the wrong message from the demise of that program. Its eighteen-month run on NBC and CBS belied the true strength of her writing. She didn't shine scripting fifteen-minute installations of an ongoing serial; all the feedback from General Mills and Blackett-Sample-Hummert should have made that clear to her. In just five years on the air Ellis managed to build an amazing level of audience loyalty and brand recognition by pitching specific products right to the consumer in her folksy, down-to-earth scripts on *Joanne Taylor's Fashion Flashes* and *The Travels of Mary Ward*. While these shows also had continuing story elements and regular characters, this is not what kept listeners tuning in, broadcast after broadcast.

Tasting success with *Caroline's Golden Store*, Ellis decided to double-down on the story aspect of her broadcasts at the expense of her salesmanship. Instead of building on the unique message delivery format she had honed as Joanne Taylor and Mary Ward, Ellis sought to stretch out into soap opera, a format in which she had no prior experience. Unfortunately, her foray into serials in the early 1940s was an unquestionable disaster for Ellis as a broadcaster, and sadly it was a wreck that didn't have to happen.

It's impossible to know, of course, where Caroline may have ended up if she had continued to perfect her own unique writing style. Maybe she would have just ended up back in Kansas City as happened anyway, but just maybe her string of lucky breaks would have continued and she could have convinced a major advertiser to give her sales-oriented programming a shot on a network hookup. In this alternate past Ellis would surely have featured much more prominently in the old-time radio histories written up to this point.

In the end Caroline Ellis may have just been the victim of unfortunate timing. She was about 55 when first introduced to the radio industry; considering the barriers to success in radio during the 1930s, that she got as far as she did with such minimal writing and performing experience is an incredible testament to her raw talent and acumen. Comfortable in her own skin and very self-assured after a lifetime of hard work, Ellis didn't prove malleable enough for the industry. Talent and confidence were crucial in achieving success on the airwaves but so was adapting to new trends and especially being willing to bend to the whims of the advertiser, the organization that ultimately signed everyone's checks. A 25- or even 35-year-old Caroline Ellis may have more readily recognized these professional necessities and found the humility to take and heed the advice of so many seasoned Chicago radio professionals.

Despite the what-ifs and could-have-beens, Ellis' two-decade radio career stands as an impressive feat in and of itself. To enter a brand new field at a late age and quickly begin earning comfortable money through the hard periods of the Depression and World War II is not an achievement of which many could boast. That she has been largely unknown in radio annals up until now is likely both a reflection of her chosen genres, homemaking and domestic sales, which have not generally been a popular area of study, and the paucity of KMBC recordings that have been in general circulation in the decades during which the old-time radio hobby has grown-up. Now that her story has been told, hopefully Caroline Ellis will receive the recognition that is long overdue.

Appendix:
Happy Home Script Selections and Summaries

The formatting and exact wording and layout of Ellis' scripts has been reproduced as closely as possible from the original material. Only obvious misspellings have been corrected.

Monday March 17, 1941

First pages of script are missing.

Bert: What about this soapmaking?

Ellis: Well, it used to be quite an event, I can tell you. This month, or next at the latest. All winter, events had been moving forward to it. Nothing said about it, since it was a part of the routine. But first, when the butchering was done and lard rendered, there were the crackling and the skins left. Of course the best of the cracklings went into that food for the gods, -- crackling corn bread. Man – man! A hunk of crackling corn bread and a glass of milk on a cold winter day! Umph! But we do get enough, in time, of anything – even food for the gods. So the rest of the cracklings and the fried out skins would go into the old washboiler set in the cellar for that purpose. And then would be added all winter long, bacon rinds, ham parings, bits of fat, all meat waste of every kind. Then along in February or March – some morning the wind would shift to the south, and boys would go to spinning tops in the sun, and the bees would come out and go to buzzing around, dandelions begin showing through, and Mrs. Farmer would say to Mr. Farmer – "John, if you'll get the kettle out in the yard for me this morning, I believe I'll make soap today and get it done with. Housecleaning'll be along before we know it." So the big iron kettle was ragged out by the wood pile, where fuel would be handy, and set up on some flat stones, level and solid and a fire kindled under it. I wonder how many people have ever known the joy of building a fire out in the open. Under the side of the kettle away from the wind, you put a few dry chips and sticks and leaves gathered from the ground around you. Behind this you crowd a piece of old paper and touch a match to it. No true lover of fire making would ever use coal oil to start with. That would spoil everything. All the suspense and the waiting – that tiny first blaze, smelling of burning leaves and dry chips, wavering, almost dying, while you watch breathlessly and blow gently – kneeling down in the dirt – feeding it with little slivers of pine and bits of bark – then finally with real wood as the smoke rolls up and the flame roars under the kettle and your fire is going at last. Building a fire in the open is one of the primitive joys of man... If you do it right ... Then the big iron kettle is filled with soft water from the cistern on the back porch. When the water is nearly boiling, lye is put in – put in until it "eats a feather." That's the expression which mean that when you dip a feather (you pick that up from the ground, too) dip a feather into the water it comes out stripped down to the stem of it. That's eating a feather. Then into this lye mixture go all the accumulated scraps – and the lye eats them up – while the grease kills the lye – the right proportions of water – lye and grease is where the science of the soap maker comes in... As the soap begins to "make" it boils up thick like molasses, and as you stir it, the bubbles – soap bubbles, white and beautiful as any that ever came from a child's bubble pipe – roll over the sides of the kettle and blow away in that soft south breeze – with all the beauty of earth in spring reflected in their shining goassamer depths ... After the soap has been boiled and tested and found just right, a shallow box is placed in basement or smoke house, lined with cloth, and into this the soap is poured, thick and foamy, and allowed to dry – then be cut into cakes and allowed to harden, And then Mrs. Farmer turns her eyes as naturally as flowers turn to the sun, toward house cleaning, and the curtain and blanket washing, which will come along about the first of May . . . Goodbye, now, until tomorrow.

Happy Home
KMBC
Caroline Ellis
8/15/45

Well, friends, it has come – the day when we can say: "It's all over." Perhaps not literally, but in intent, war has ceased. There is no war in all the world today! Let's say that over again – and slowly, so as to savor it as fully as it's possible for us to. The world is free today – free of war. In all the world there is no war – not in Europe – nor in Asia – not in England – not in Greece – nor in the Near East – nor on any of the seven seas. Someway it makes it more real to name the places. Quiet, at last. When I came out on the street this morning at a little after six o'clock, the world was grey, a cool, quiet grey. The streets at that unusually busy corner were empty of any living soul except myself. The air was cool and crisp, like a drink of fresh spring water. I stood there a few moments and listened. Only distant sounds. And into my mind flowed the lines: "The tumult and the shouting dies – The captains and the kings depart." I was sorry my memory failed me at the next line, but all the way down town my mind kept saying: "A humble and a contrite heart." Yes, friends, a humble and contrite heart. Now that the tumult and the shouting are over – it is time to be humble and contrite that we, the people of the earth ever allowed the world to get into such a shape that it took all the destruction and all the pain and dying to begin to start to set it right again. For today, the first day of world peace is only a chance for us to begin to have peace. That's all. I wonder how you heard the great news. Of course, we folks who are close to radio knew that something was coming – and when. So about five o'clock, I got my car out of the garage, picked up a friend and we drove north – out of the city, out over the hills and through the valleys, driving slowly with the radio on – Someway I wanted it to be that way. I wanted that moment to be quiet. A few minutes before six o'clock, we stopped the car on the summit of a high hill. We didn't plan it that way. It just seemed to be the thing to do. And there, in the silence, with the horizon stretching open and far on every side we heard the news. The news we waited for so long.

That war is over. By the magic of radio we heard the cheer go up in Washington – we heard the tremble in the voice of the announcer who read the phrases of that momentous document – the phrases of a vanquished foe. Even while the joy of the moment tightened my throat and misted my eyes, I thought what it must be like for a proud and arrogant ruler to say: "I am through!" I will fight no more. I will do whatever you say for me to do. That fate, thank God, has never come to this nation. And let us pray that we may never invite it, by an act of oppression or arrogance or covetousness of lack of friendship for our neighbors on the earth. Of course, when the moment had passed, then we wanted to get back to share in the joy of others. So back to the city we sped as fast as we thought we could drive. But all the way back over and over in my thoughts beat the words: "They who live by the sword must perish by the sword." Surely if ever that has come true in the world's history, it has come true in our time. Those who live by the sword – violence is not God's way. It is never the plan to progress and those who seek to make it so must and will in time, perish. That is our lesson. And if we Have not learned that lesson, then we, too, will be doomed. Even today, when it seems that surely we may take a little time to rejoice, let us set about making peace work. As the days follow on – the blessed days of reconstructing our lives and the world, let us never forget that nothing is settled – unless it is settled with us – in us. That there will never be any real peace unless WE make it. A humble and a contrite heart. And so we take up our lives again on this 15th day of August, 1945. With prayer and thanksgiving ... with a firm resolve that those who had to give their lives to bring us this day, shall not have given in vain ... That would be our unpardonable sin – to want only require of our young and our best to risk and to give our lives – to die the death of violence – and all for nothing. That sin, I think God Himself could not forgive us.

****

I had another thought yesterday as we drove back to the city – a thought of another woman. We heard commentator after commentator pay his tribute to Franklin Roosevelt, and the great part he played in our final victory. Paying the tribute due to him, even though he passed from the scene before the end came for which he planned and worked toward which he so valiantly lead us. But do you know who it was I was thinking of? Eleanor Roosevelt! Where was she? What were her thoughts? Eleanor Roosevelt is too big a woman to have known any bitterness. But surely she would not be human if all the tumult and the shouting did not bring to her the thought – that she, too, along with millions of other women over the world – that she, too, is a widow of this war ... Goodbye, my friends, until tomorrow.

Happy Home
Thurs. March 9, 1950
9:30 to 9:45 AM

ANNCR: It's 9:30 and time again for the Happy Home with Caroline Ellis, brought to you today by WINDEX SPRAY ... W-I-N-D-E-X ... WINDEX ... the glass cleaner that has revolutionized window cleaning: no mess, no dust ... spray a little on ... wipe it off ... your windows sparkle! That's Windex spray. Get a bottle today! Caroline –

Ellis: Thank you David – and I will. After all this dust blowing, my windows have to have it. And how are you today, my friends? Before we take a dive into the deep south this morning, here is something important in the education of girls that I want to say just a few words about. It is the Home Economics in Business Field Day that is being held in Kansas City tomorrow. You know how I have always recommended the study of Home Economics for girls going to colleges – because it is a branch of study from which can lead to business paths which can take a career girl most anywhere she wants to go. And that is what this day, tomorrow is for – to acquaint college sophomores and Juniors with the types of work, working conditions, the availability of jobs and surroundings, to be found in home economics jobs with business firms here in Kansas City. That is, what jobs and all about them, there are here in Kansas City which it takes knowledge of Home Economics to fill. And there will be over 100 college girls and instructors from approximately 17 colleges gathered here, tomorrow for this Field Day. At the morning session in the Power and Light Building, Mrs. Nell Nichols, Field Representative of Women's Home Companion, from Topeka, Kansas, will speak to the girls on "Stepping from

College into business." Mr. Rod Cupp of KMBC Radio Station will speak on "The Future of Home Economics in Business." There will be a fashion show: "Fashions in Careers." There will be a luncheon where Mrs. Mary B. Horton of Sealtest Consumer Service Department, located in New York, will speak on "America's Business is Women's Business." In the afternoon a tour of big industries of Kansas City and a dinner in the evening. It will be a big day for these college girls specializing in Home Economics. And should show them they have done well in their choice of a career ... Now we roll out the magic carpet. Whisk! ... and we're even south of Miami and still going south. Of course we stop at Fairchild Garden, but we'll leave that for some time in the future. Here we are, driving along a jungle you can't see into – though we hear strange caws and shatterings. Here is a largish curio shop and over the top – PARROT JUNGLE. We're admitted at a gate beside the curio shop – and immediately you can't believe your eyes – nor your ears, either. Now, remember, when I say parrot, I may mean macaw, or parakeet, or cockatoo – and it's not to be charged against me. For whatever they are, you can't believe them. Right there they were, in a sort of open space back of the shop, used for exhibition purposes. And there must have been nearly a hundred – scattered from the low bushes up to the towering forest trees. And such a going on. And believe it or not, in the center stood a young chap about 20, maybe, who calls those flashes of living color by name, from as far as the bird could hear him – here it would come. Imagine calling a parrot – by its name – from the very top branch of a giant cypress or a pin oak. Not one parrot but dozens. [*Script damage prevents reading next two lines*] to settle on the young man's shoulder. He'd say – But where's Maggie – oh, there she is. You come, too, Maggie – I've got something for you. Of course the something was a nut of some kind. Peanut, likely. The birds do all parrot stunts ... I can't tell them all. These magnificent birds are bred and raised right there. I'd judge the place had been there for at least 25 years. We were told that parrots do not mate until they are 10 years old – I tried to look that up after I came back but couldn't find anything on it – but once mated they are monogamous. The keepers there try to mate them so as to bring more and more vivid and strange coloring, and they think they have been pretty successful – though they say sometimes the individual birds will not accept the mate chosen for them. Parrots live to old age, sometimes as old as 70 years. In a tree was a pair which took no part in the exhibition – we were told they were new – had been purchased at a good sum – I forget whether it was hundreds or thousands of dollars. They attracted gasps of wonder at their beauty – for they were almost solid rich, brilliant navy blue. Visitors exclaimed they had never seen such color before. After the exhibition, we went out through the jungle, but I assure you we didn't find our own way. There were lanes cut through with clipped bark to walk on and again roofed over head with the everlasting jungle. I feel sure I was not the only person there who have a thought to our boys in the jungle fighting of the war. How did it happen a single one came out alive. Through the jungle there were cages of parrots – of pheasants – and the strange crowned pigeons – which I am sure not many of you have ever seen. And then we finally came out of the jungle into the sunshine. And I'll tell you what we saw after that … AFTER I've told you something which will be of great benefit to you here at home.

****

This is about Windex Spray – which most of us are needing very much at this time. Now Windex Spray is the easiest way known to clean windows sparkling clean. Usually, all you do is just spray it on, with the little spray that comes with the bottle. Then wipe it off – presto, your windows sparkle. But I don't have to tell you women in this region what has happened recently. First, dust storms out of the southwest. Then – a bit of rain – a bit of snow – and very cold. I know my windows are in very bad shape indeed Now, this is how I manage it. First off, you wouldn't want to use a window cleaner that would shower more dust on top of that already on your window sills even if this dust might be white. You don't want to make things worse. You want Windex Spray that leaves no dust – no mess – just cleans. Here is what I've done. In this emergency I give my windows a double dose of Windex Spray – mainly to save my clean white rags. I spray Windex on good. Then I take paper towels and go over the whole glass and get off what grime I can on those paper towels. And after that, I found that just a thin spraying of Windex – over all – a wiping with my clean white rags, and my windows – well, I was proud of them. I really was. It didn't seem possible they could look so pretty after that awful dust we had and the snow, too. I do advise you to try that same thing, friends. You can get Windex spray at any drug or grocery store. The small bottle is only 15 cents, but in this case I think you'd better get the larger bottles. You may need it and it's always good to have on hand. While you're there, pick up a can of Drano, too – made by the same company. Both Windex Spray and Drano are being featured this week at the Associated Grocers Stores. And so – bright sparkling windows to you, too!

****

Well, we came out of the dark and exotic jungle into the clear sunshine. And there were peacocks parading and spreading their tails, in the edge of the clearing, and I was amused to hear the young man conducting – he had gone out with us from the city – tell the crowd these were the females strutting to attract a mate. In my own helpful way I explained to him his error. His face was very red. And there inside rock walls were white swans and tall cranes in a little lake with an island in the center ... and on we went – this is a big place this Parrot Jungle – and so we came to another larger lake, also rock wall enclosed. And all around was the bougainvillea in three colors ... and on this second lake were the black swans – slow and mystical. And on the green grass of the lake shore, probably 30 to 40 pink flamingos. The black swans, the blue water, the green grass, the pink flamingoes – all in the bright sunshine. You could hear the people "oh-h-" as one person. Flamingoes are pretty, even exquisite. But forgive me if I say to me they are very stupid. It was the Red Queen, wasn't it, who tucked one under her arm and used its long neck and head as a croquet mallet? To me, that seems most fitting, and I laughed as I remembered that while looking at them. They stand asleep in the sun, literally, I'm sure, for hours. Stand on one slender and stiff and stick-like leg and never move. What they do with that other leg I can't figure. Since it is so long I can't see how it can be hidden from sight among the pink feathers. And that terrifically long neck. It's a sight to see them dispose of that neck as they prepare for their hours long sleep. You see, they have too much neck, really. For they put their head and bill back flat on top of their shoulders, tucked between their wings where the wings join the body. Now, that neck is considerably too long for that. It would hang in a loop and things might catch in it. So – to dispose of that length of neck, they give their neck a sort of acrobatic twist, putting an S curve in that loop – then up over their shoulder and sock, goes their head between the main joint of their wings and they're set for hours. I'm sure young flamingoes must need to be taught the acrobatics of going to sleep. Well, there was an overpass in the road here, and over on the other side was a park, again in a rock wall. The park was a steep slope – covered with flowers – shrubs – and away down there at the bottom of the slope over on the far side… I haven't told you yet of the Australian pine which Florida has adopted and made her own and uses it beyond words. This pine is not a pretty tree alone. Its foliage is thin. Its needles are in bunches, smaller than a broom straw, jointed like cane. Its beauty is in the mass, when this thin foliage makes it soft – almost feathery looking. Its usefulness is in its rapid growth. It is planted for windbreaks – for shield from the sun … it is planted six to eight inches apart like picket fences, sawed off at 6 to 8 feet vines grow over it. Australian pine down there grows a foot and a half in a year – in favorable soil will grow three feet a year. You see it everywhere. In the mass and at a distance it takes on a dark green almost somber mysterious depth. It looks as if, could you press your hand against it, it would feel soft like green feathers, or green pillows, maybe. Well, away down yonder at the other side of that park, at the foot of the slope, on the other side of a little stream, and against that stone wall, were these Australian Pine. A grove of them – a miniature forest of them. Away below us, but in full view. At that distance they could be from any fairy book – they didn't belong in today. They were somber and mysterious and deep – I didn't listen to the guide any more. I guess I have a peculiar mind. For I looked and looked and looked at that fairy land forest, and imagined if all at once a herd of unicorns might come marching proudly out, or a troop of armoured knights riding richly caparisoned steeds. It could have been, you know. That was the very place for those things – it would have been perfectly fitting. Well, I had to wake up then, and

I'll have to wake up now. But it was something while it lasted. Now, friends, tonight at the well known address of 1020 McGee St, room 600, you'll have another chance to get a Chest X-Ray, free of charge – through the Kansas City Tuberculosis Society. Any time between 5:30 and 8 o'clock tonight. Now, please let me make it plain that you do not need an appointment for this. Just go to the 6th floor of the YWCA Building, 1020 McGee, after 5:30 and before 8 this evening. Get your chest X-Ray free of any charge. Goodbye, now, until tomorrow.

ANNCR: Goodbye, Caroline . . . Friends, if you haven't tried Windex Spray for cleaning your windows, try it now. You can have no idea how easily it will clean those windows left dirty by our recent dust storms. Remember, too, the makers of Windex Spray also make Drano, that wonder product that cleans out clogged-up drains. Get a can of Drano, too. The Happy Home with Caroline Ellis is heard each weekday at this time, presented today by the makers of Windex Spray and Drano, two products essential to the modern sanitary home. Also participating in the Happy Home is Celanese Corporation of America.

Happy Home
Saturday March 7, 1953
8:30 - 8:45 AM

ANNCR: It's 8:30 and time for the Happy Home with Caroline Ellis, women's commentator, news and views of the week. Caroline---

Ellis: Thank you . . . Good morning, David. And how are you today, my friends. Say, David – have you been away somewhere?

Well, we've had quite a bit of snow in these parts recently. It isn't every year that we see nine inches of snow on the ground here. As the weather men told us there was, in the two storms. I know I've not seen snow pile up on the outside window sills before. And it did this time. Nor long icicles reaching from the upper sash to the lower. And never a more beautiful sight than the thick snow fall, athwart the wide windows there up on the bluff. I don't like cold weather – I don't like anything about it – except the falling snow. After it has fallen I want nothing to do with it, at all. When I listened to the weather prediction yesterday morning, warning of a cold wave – more snow – I thought of the days on the farm when a weather warning such as that would come. Over the telegraph wires, often – and then out over the party line. A cold wave was coming. Protect your stock. That was before the days of silos. The farmer hearing the news would grab his cap – the one with the earflaps – and his gloves – grab his jacket – still putting it on he'd hurry out – calling to his son – or the hired man – "There's a cold wave on the way. We better get in some fodder." Everything would be dropped – the farmer would call back – "Get the hay rack on the wagon. I'll harness up." Soon I'd hear the light rumble of the wagon wheels, the rattle of the empty hay rack – the loud voices of the men, talking against the rising wind. Out in the field you'd see them working rapidly – against the storm that was already beating in. Loading the shocks of fodder. Around the barn and the feed lot, the cattle were already milling and lowing. Back from the field comes the load, light snow blinding the men and the horses – quickly they unload – then turn back toward the field again. The woman goes to the door – calls – "you're not going back again. In this storm that's coming?" The farmer grins – looks around – says: "I'd say it's already coming. And it's gonna be a dandy –" He flicks the lines – the horses break into a trot. The farmer and the sailor. Children of nature . . . Well, I guess there's no doubt as to the head line of this week. If I should ask you, without doubt the answer would be unanimous. Stalin is Dead. Of course I have no prognostication to add to that, such as various world commentators – and world statesmen would have. Though I have an idea that anything I might say would be of about as much value – at this time. For who knows anything. Of course, like all of you, I heard the news several times Thursday night – Stalin is dead. So that when I picked up my paper outside my door yesterday morning I knew what would be there. But I didn't expect it to be so big – letters clear across the page. So I sat in my chair and drank my coffee and stared at the headline and thought. Would the headline have been any bigger if our own president had died in the night? Or the young Queen Elizabeth? Or any sovereign throughout all the world? Why was it? Why did his death merit all this publicity? Was it a stoppage of progress – the end of happiness, perhaps – for whole peoples? A great and irretrievable loss? We know what it was – a new fear. What now? Are we more free from the danger of a world destroying war? – or are we closer to it. How strange that a man can, in one lifetime, build up such power over other humans who might be considered to be on a par with himself. Power that builds in others the strongest emotion mankind is capable of . . . Fear. Fear that is stronger than love or happiness . . . that makes subjects of all. So that even nations like the United States and Britain cannot move – or do not – without asking: What will Stalin think of this – what will be Russia's – which is Stalin's – reaction be. It's all grotesque – and has been. One man – over the world. Another thing to think about. Dictators come from the people themselves. In our own time – Hitler – a house painter and paper hanger. Stalin whose father was a cobbler – in the far away little state of Georgia. Yet Hitler set the world aflame with horror and Stalin rose to the Kremlin and held power of life and death over 800,000,000 people and threw fear across the world. But Hitler killed himself and Stalin is dead. Yesterday morning, Kalterborn, the commentator, said One dictator is never succeeded by another dictator – the first only word of hope I have heard. While we wait to see, we can have a lot to think about . . . And we should – trying to see beyond what happens and why it happened . . . We seem to have been granted here a little while of freedom from tension. I think it would not be seemly to start a war until the remains are properly laid away. However, who knows? . . . Well, well, let's look around in our dooryard. I have here a very interesting letter. From Mrs. Robert Geppert, Secretary of the Greater Kansas City Foundation for Exceptional Children. President Dr. C. G. Leitch. The letter says: Dear Miss Ellis: Our group is a non-profit, non-sectarian organization dedicated to aid the retarded child, and we raise funds for our cause by bake sales, rummage sales, card parties and donations. As part of our program we operate a training school for exceptional children at 4125 Troost. There are thirty-five children who are not permitted in the public school system, enrolled there and more are on the waiting list. We have four teachers and a speech therapist. At present we are sponsoring a rummage sale to be held March 20 and 21 (dates) at 1206 E. 12th St. But because of the bad weather this week we have had a slow response to our drive (we can well believe that) our drive for used clothing, dishes, bric-a-brac, jewelry, etc. We need your help. Would you please announce this drive on your radio program? Anyone having rummage can call Mrs. S. D. MacFarlane, Je. 9024 or Mrs. E. E. Poulter, Benton 7980. We are earnestly trying to make this benefit a success . . . I know many of you will be interested immediately on hearing this letter. The names I gave you may be found in the telephone book, in case you did not quite get the telephone numbers where you may call. The names again are: GIVE NAMES AND PHONE NUMBERS . . .

I see that the members of Kansas City Chapter of Sweet Adelines, Inc. are going to sing in the Little Theater tonight, starting at 8:00 PM. The Sweet Adelines are the feminine angle of the Barber Shop singing movement, as you might say. However, as I understand it they are a separate organization. Anyway, they are well worth hearing, as many will testify. For you – if any – who haven't protected your interests, musically speaking by getting tickets well in advance of the dates of the coming opera season, remember the first La Boheme opera will be the nights of the 12th and 14th – and that's next week. At this first opera you will hear Jan Peerce, tenor, and Tenor from the Metropolitan Opera in New York, who will sing the role of Rudolfo . . . and Irma Gonzales star soprano of the National Theater of Mexico, in the role of Mimi. I anticipate a fine evening, myself. Tickets by mail and also over the counter may still be had at the Philharmonic box office, 209 Altman Building, Mr. Walter Fritschy, who is ticket manager of the Opera Festival said. However, as you can figure for yourself, time is of the essence. And it's running out . . .

Happy Home Script Summaries

Surviving scripts of Caroline Ellis' twenty years on the airwaves are surprisingly sparse. Considering she aired multiple times a week for so long from larger stations in Kansas City, Des Moines, and Chicago and even had a show on NBC and CBS, nearly every one of her few surviving scripts is preserved in a collection held by her family. The KMBC and NBC archives appear to be void of any such documents.

March 17, 1941

Description of traditional soap making.

September 15, 1942

A philosophical reflection on things Caroline hates, including those who exploit others and racial prejudice.

September 17, 1942
Daily commentary, 2:15 – 2:30

Caroline discussed the area of Suez, then in the news because of war headlines. The broadcast covered the area's geography, people, and vast history.

September 23, 1942

Caroline discusses anti-English comments made by author Theodore Dreiser.

October 10, 1942

Caroline takes a look at the life of Margaret Wilson, daughter of former president Woodrow Wilson. In her later years Wilson became a Hindu nun in India and died sixteen months after this broadcast on February 12, 1944.

October 22, 1942 (mistakenly dated 1952)

Caroline "visits" the Mediterranean island of Malta. She expounds on the area's long history, from the time of the ancient Phoenicians to the (then) current World War II. Fran Heyser announcer.

April 13, 1945

Caroline delivers a heavy tribute to President Franklin D. Roosevelt who died the day before. She focuses especially on Roosevelt's widow, Eleanor Roosevelt.

August 15, 1945

Caroline reflects on the worldwide joy in the wake of Japan's surrender; It's a joy born out of great suffering and pain. She listened to the news while looking to the horizon from atop a hill outside of the city.

Happy Home with Caroline Ellis
8:30 – 8:45
Sponsored by Celanese Corporation of America (some days sustaining)

March 5, 1946
Caroline discusses the excitement of Winston Churchill's visit to Westminster College in Fulton, MO, where he gave a historic speech formally titled "Sinews of Peace" but more often referred to as the "Iron Curtain Speech." She broadcast via remote from Fulton.

May 6, 1946
This broadcast featured a history of Silkville, a utopian communal society founded in northeastern Kansas by Frenchmen ca. 1870. Ellis shares a conversation she had with Anna Laura Bitts Frits who lived in Silkville as a girl.

May 17, 1946 (Sustaining)
Caroline wryly notes the seeming abundance of new cars on city streets, despite repeated claims that civilians should not expect much availability of new autos for some time.

May 20, 1946
Caroline reflects on the public's reaction to the wife of Major Hans Hornbostel's becoming ill with leprosy. She went to seek treatment in Carville, LA, home of the nation's first leprosarium, or "leper colony." Ellis was taken aback by the seeming "superstition" that still surrounded that ancient disease. Ellis goes on to provide some background about the public health fight against leprosy.

November 10, 1947
Caroline spends the entire broadcast exploring jade in depth, including its physical properties and how it has been utilized by humans through the centuries.

9:30 – 9:45

October 26, 1948
After an announcement about an upcoming collector's auction at the Kansas City Art Institute to benefit the scholarship fund of the Fireside Committee, Caroline expounds on pearls. She covers their history, how they are harvested, and their use by humans over history. Sponsored by S.C. Johnson and Son products ca. 1949.

March 7, 1950 (Sponsor product: Drano)
Upon returning from a Southern trip the day before, Caroline reminisces on bad weather in New Orleans and the beauty of Miami.

March 8, 1950 (Sponsor: Celanese Corp.)
A series of broadcasts takes Caroline's listeners on an audio tour of the American South, including stops in Memphis, Birmingham, and Atlanta. This episode features a quick tour of Florida, which focuses on the state's trees and Biscayne Bay. The show travels from Jacksonville to Miami.

March 9, 1950 (Sponsor products: Windex and Drano)
Caroline looks ahead to the Home Economics in Business Field Day that will be held in Kansas City the next day at the city's Power and Light building. She then turns to discussing a stop at a curio shop called Parrot Jungle on her recent Florida trip.

March 10, 1950 (Sponsor product: Celanese Corp., acetate yarn)
Caroline takes her listeners on an audio tour of the Florida Everglades. She describes both the geography and history of the area, with a focus on the Seminole and Osceola Native American tribes and escaped slaves.

8:30 – 8:45

January 10, 1953
Caroline is excited by the recent discovery of the coelacanth, an ancient fish that filled in a gap in the evolutionary tree. She takes the listener on a 300-million-year journey using Rachel Carson's "The Sea Around Us" to explain the origin of all life in the sea. She marvels at the evolutionary process.

March 7, 1953 (sustaining, "news and views of the week")
A nine-inch snowfall has buried Kansas City but the big news is the recent death of Joseph Stalin, who "held power of life and death over 800,000,000 people." Locally, The Greater Kansas City Foundation for Exceptional Children is raising funds for its training school and the Kansas City chapter of Sweet Adelines, Inc. was performing at the Little Theater. The school enrolled 35

children who were not allowed to attend public schools due to various disabilities.

Undated:
Farm Hour (6:00 – 6:45)

Recipes and instructions to:
- Can sweet potatoes
- Bake stuffed sweet potatoes
- Make sweet potatoes au gratin
- Make scalloped sweet potatoes and apples
- Make sweet potato nut croquettes
- Bake sweet potato pie

Typical advertising copy from this era of Ellis' programs:

"Now, it's going to be nice to talk about my produce, Celanese, again. And whatever styles of blouses you're planning to buy ... however much or little you're planning to spend, remember this blouse buying tip that most smartly dressed women know. They want blouses that stay pretty with a minimum of care. So they make sure the blouse fabric is woven of Celanese acetate rayon yarn. That's the way to pick blouses that are a breeze to wash and iron ... and dry extra fast.

They feel wonderful to wear, too ... and come in especially flattering colors ... and in white that stays white. For example – there's a new Ann Todd blouse ... picture in March Charm Magazine. You'll find it at J. S. Lerner's Vogue Shops, and at Miller-Wohl ... in sizes 32-38, priced at ONLY $3. It's made of a Tanbro fabric ... a smooth rich crepe woven of Celanese acetate yarn. The style is on the dressy side ... with a graceful cut-out neckline ... filled in with shadowy net ... and topped with a Peter Pan collar. Choose this pretty blouse ... to wear now and later ... in gleaming white, aqua, deep or pale pink. Look for this Ann Todd blouse, in a fabric of Celanese acetate yarn, at J. S. Lerner's Vogue Shops and at Miller-Wohl. Celanese is a registered trademark of Celanese Corporation of America.

Poetry Selections

As with the scripts above, the formatting and text of these selected poems has been reproduced as closely as possible from the original written material. Only obvious typographical errors have been corrected.

One-Ness

(originally published in the *Kansas City Post*)

Today I drove the cattle down to the creek to drink,
Today, between the sun's setting and the twilight:
The cattle drank of the water – the clear, shining mirror-water,
I stood on the bank above . . . .
A silence struck through to my consciousness, and I awoke . . . . . .
Nothing moved: the trees – the grass – the leaves – the sky – the water – the cattle standing in the water – the birds – the universe – the worm at my feet –
Only my wide, seeing eyes moved.
And God answered: "For you to know that you – the earth under your feet – the cattle in the water – the bird against the cloud – the caterpillar in the leaf – and myself – all – all are kin."
And I said: "God, I know."

The Wise Man

(Originally published in the *Kansas City Post*)

And I came upon a man.
And he was seated upon the ground.
And his body rocked to the rhythm of his wailing.
His head was grey with ashes.
His garment of horse hair tore at his flesh.
And I said, "Why mournest thou, unhappy one?"
And he made answer between his wailings: "It is that I repent me grievously of my sin."
And I said, "What sin hast thou done, accursed of God?"
And he answered, "I have done no sin."
"Dost thou make a mock of me, fool?" I cried. "Thou hast done no sin and yet thou repentest of thy sin! What foolishness is this?
And his body ceased to rock and his voice to wail while

he made answer: "It is true that I have done no sin. I had conceived my sin, and it rode upon my fancy so that I knew in truth I should do it. And as all sin bringeth repentance in its train, it is my custom to repent first, that the memory of my repentance shall eat up the lust for my sin. In this wise do I alone suffer and none other."
And he raised his voice anew and his body rocked with his wailing. And I cast myself into the dust before him and besought him that I might sit at his feet.

Saturday Night Blues In An Apartment House

Radio – radio --------
"Ramona –"
"I gotta go where you are –"
"There's a Rainbow Round My Shoulders –"
(Where is that wailing saxophone –
Whah-whah-whah-whah--)
The pulse of dancing feet –
Thump-thump-thump-thump-
Shrill laughter – too shrill –
"Wait a minute! Wa-a-it a minute!
Gawd, you work fast."
"And that's my weakness, now."
(Whah-whah-whah-o-o-oh --)
"My god, ain't it hot!
"Somebody open a window someplace fur Christ's sake."
"Any you guys called the bootlegger?
"This-a las' bottl' ---"
(Where is that saxophone!
Whah-whah-whah-whah-o-o-o-oh!
Whah-whah-whah-whah-o-o-o-oh!
How human a saxophone can sound.
Ever hear the Farewell Blues?)
A fight somewhere –
"I seen yu' –
"I heard yu' –
"I got the goods on yu' this time, yu' dirty –"

"What's the diff'runce if I say I'll go away
"When I'll come back on my knees someday –"
(Now there's two saxophones –
Base – contralto –
Not so loud, ow – kind of soft –
Whah – whah – whah –
O-o-o-o-o-o-o-o-o-o-o------)
"The sun shines bright, the world's all right –"
Then through a lighted window across the area-way I see them –
The saxophones –
One on one side of a bed and one on the other –
Base and contralto saxophones –
And between them something small and white and very still –
"Sonny Boy --- Sonny Boy –"

My Beloved - an Allegory

Today I am making Water Melon Preserves,
Delicious Preserves made from the Rind of the Riper Watermelon.
They have done beautifully.
They came from the kettle
Inch cubes of deep transparent cream
Tinged with tenderest green and tipped with crimson
Each dripping luscious golden syrup –
A Pastoral in color.
I am most fond of this Preserve,
Made from the Rind of the Ripe Watermelon.
Yet I eat of it sparingly –
A little bit today, a little bit tomorrow
Thus shall I not lose my Joy in eating the Preserve
Made from the Rind of the Ripe Watermelon.
But did I know that never from today –
That never but on this one day would come to me
This – to me – one supreme delight,
Then would I put from me every other appetite,
And on this one day would eat and eat of the Preserve
Made from the Rind of the Ripe Watermelon,
And so would gain Satiety,

And with it –
Peace.

Exotic

Twelfth and Main – noon
Hot – hot as hell –
Wind in the south –
Traffic jam – drivers cursing – brakes screeching – horns blaring.
Little ants of humanity running – scuttling –
Fear driven – whip driven – law driven –
And through it all wanders idly
A big black man –
Loose jointed –
Huge framed –
Jungle gaited –
Overalls and jumper –
Moving aimlessly – ambling
A giant black man –
Twirling in his great fingers
A single red, red rose.

To My Young Lover

Dim the light, Beloved, one short hour –
Shut out the slanderous light – o, shut it out –
That you may see no more
The face that feels your bosom's rise and fall:
That you may no more see
The body lying prone for your caress.
Leave just one ray – one little ray –
To strike across my eyes.
Then in them lock – such a little way –
And I shall spring to meet you – I
Who hide all day in this ill-fitting house.
I shall come forth all naked as I am,
- Vibrant, eager, young and passion mad.
Then
Love me – love me – with your lips and limbs,

There is no bit of me but sobs for you.
Bend down your mouth, Beloved, let me drink –
Your springs are at their full, and Oh, I thirst.
Fold tight your arms – hold me so close and warm
That I shall fail to hear the autumn wind
Which moans and whimpers just outside my door.

Bibliography

Archival Material

Arthur B. Church Papers, 1885-1980, Special Collections Department, Parks Library, Iowa State University.

Arthur B. Church KMBC Radio Collection (Manuscripts), LaBudde Special Collections, Miller Nichols Library, University of Missouri-Kansas City.

Arthur B. Church KMBC Radio Collection (Audiovisual), Marr Sound Archives, Miller Nichols Library, University of Missouri-Kansas City.

Crockett Family Papers.

Kansas City Museum/Union Station Archives, Union Station, Kansas City, MO.

Missouri Valley Special Collections, Kansas City Public Library, Kansas City, MO.

Ted Malone Collection, LaBudde Special Collections, Miller Nichols Library, University of Missouri-Kansas City.

Books

Anthony, Lenore. *Whimsies*. Kansas City: Lowell Press, 1928.

Baker, John C. *Farm Broadcasting: The First Sixty Years*. Ames, IA: The Iowa State University Press, 1981.

Birkby, Robert. *KMA Radio: The First Sixty Years*. Shenandoah, IA: May Broadcasting Company, 1985.

Cox, Jim. *Frank and Anne Hummert's Radio Factory: The Programs and Personalities of Broadcasting's Most Prolific Producers*. Jefferson, NC: McFarland & Company, 2003.

-----. *The Great Radio Soap Operas*. Jefferson, NC: McFarland & Company, 1999.

Douglas, Susan J. *Listening In: Radio and the American Imagination, from Amos 'n' Andy and Edward R. Murrow to Wolfman Jack and Howard Stern*. NY: Times Books, 1999.

Dunning *On the Air: The Encyclopedia of Old-Time Radio*. New York: Oxford University Press, 1998.

Ellett, Ryan. *Radio Drama and Comedy Writers, 1928-1962*. Jefferson, NC: McFarland & Company, 2017.

-----. *The Texas Rangers: Two Decades on Radio, Film, Television, and Stage*. Albany, GA: BearManor Media, 2014.

Halper, Donna L. *Invisible Stars: A Social History of Women in American Broadcasting*. New York: M. E. Sharpe, 2014.

Kleber, John E. (Editor in Chief). *The Kentucky Encyclopedia*. Lexington, KY: The University of Kentucky Press, 1992.

Hilmes, Michele. *Radio Voices: American Broadcasting, 1922-1952*. Minneapolis, University of Minnesota Press, 1997.

Hilmes, Michele and Jason Loviglio. *Radio Reader: Essays in the Cultural History of Radio*. NY: Routledge, 2002.

Sies, Leora M. and Luther F. Sies. *The Encyclopedia of Women in Radio, 1920-1960*. Jefferson, NC: McFarland & Company, 2012.

Theses & Dissertations

Armstrong, Kara. "Women of Kansas City: Theatre Mentors." Thesis. University of Missouri - Kansas City, 2004.

Articles

Kiddle, Bill. "Old Time Radio Series Reviews." *Old Time Radio Digest* (#113, 2006).

McCormic, John. "Caroline Ellis Wins Title Role in New WHO Production." *Rural Radio* (#1, 1938).

Newspapers

Chanute Daily Tribune (Chanute, KS)
Chicago Tribune
Daily Independent (Hutchinson, KS)
Hutchinson News (Hutchinson, KS)
Iola Register (Iola, KS)
Kansas City Globe (Kansas City, KS)
Kansas City Kansan (Kansas City, KS)
Leavenworth Times (Kansas City, KS)
Republic City News (Republic City, KS)
Salina Daily Union (Salina, KS)
Topeka State Journal (Topeka, KS)

Magazines

Billboard
Broadcasting
Indiana Medical Journal
Indiana School Journal and Teacher
Kansas Historical Society
Motion Picture Herald
Radio Broadcasting News
Radio Daily
Radio Digest
Radio Mirror
Radio Showmanship
Radiocast Weekly
Variety
*Wireless Age*eAce, Goodman 13, 42

Index

Adams, Guila 57, 59
Advertising Club of Kansas City 29
All City High School Radio Workshop, The (Kansas City) 89
Allsweet Margarine 43
Alpha Delta Sigma 87
amateur radio ix
American Meat Institute 87
American Radio and Research Company (AMRAD) x
American Story 86
Amos Parrish & Co. 27
Anderson, Gwen 50
Anderson, James (see Crockett, Asher) 1
Andrews, David 85-86
Andrus, Naoma 23
Anthony, Lenore 20-25
Army Air Corps 86
Arnold Grimm's Daughter 59, 63
"Art Lesson, The" 92, 94
Arthur B. Church Productions 50, 95
Association of Women Radio Directors 90
Aunt Jane xiv
Backstage Wife 59
Barger, Sarabeth 50
Barnum, Margaret 20
Battle of the Alamo 1
Beck, Loretta 86
Behrens, Frank 57
Bennett, Sam 95
Berle, Milton 13
Bernfield, Bernie 31
Bethany College (West Virginia) 5
Betty and Bob 58
Betty Crocker Gold Medal Flour Home Service Talk xiii
Between the Bookends 36
"Beulah Kearney's Kitchen Hints" 41

Beverly Hillbillies, The 14
Billboard 35, 87
Bingham, Harry 50, 53, 60
Birkby, Robert xiii
Bisquick 59
Bits from the Classics 22
Blackett-Sample-Hummert 48, 50, 52, 54, 55, 57, 63, 64, 66-67, 68, 69, 101
Blair, Roland 27
Blankenship, Sarah 1
Blue Cross 100
Book of Knowledge, The 22
Bracegirdle, The 8
Bren, Ruth Lee 20, 21
Brighter Day, The xv
Brinkley, Jack 57
Browne, R. Edwin 89
Brush Creek Follies 86
Bryson, Dr. Lyman 94
Bullock's Department Store 30
Burton, O. D. 9
Butler College (Indiana) 5
Butternut Coffee 50
Calavo Subtropic Fruit Co. 42, 43
Calling Barbara Winthrop 58
Camp Fire Girls, The 18
Cannon, Winnifred 87, 88
Carl, Cliff 50, 55, 57, 58, 59
Caroline's Golden Store 45-69, 70, 71, 72, 75, 76, 91, 97, 100, 101,
Carrington, Elaine xv, 75
Carters of Elm Street, The 59
CBS (Columbia Broadcasting System) 12, 13, 14, 43, 45, 59, 89, 94, 95, 100, 115
CBS American School of the Air 89, 92, 93
Celanese Corporation of American 84

Chamberlain Hotel (Des Moines, IA) 48
Chatham Blankets (New York) 33
Chef Boy-Ar-Dee's Spaghetti Dinner 43
Church, Arthur B. 12-14, 26, 27, 36, 37, 38, 41, 42, 45, 48, 49-50, 53-54, 55, 63, 64, 66, 69, 75, 76, 77, 89, 91, 94, 95, 96, 98
Church, Dr. Charles F. 92, 94
Cirotto, George (see Andrews, David)
City College of New York 91
Civil War (United States) 2
Civilian Conservation Corps 86
Classic Hour 15
Coffee Pot Inn 50
Como, Perry 13
Compton, Robin D. 95
Convention of National Retail Dry Goods (1939) 35
Cook Paint and Varnish Company 98
Cook, Aubry Waller 14, 15
Cooking School xiv
Cool, Gomer 13
Cox, Jim xv
Creighton University 90
Crocker, Betty xiv, 55, 65
Crockett, Asher 1
Crockett, Beam 4
Crockett, Caroline Matilda 2
Crockett, David Stern 1
Crockett, Louis Albert 2
Crockett, Minnie Gertrude 2, 9-10, 26
Crockett, Peter Marshall 1
Crockett, Robert Marshall 2
Crockett, Stephen Marshall 4, 5, 6
Crockett, Steve 4
Crowley, Milner and Company 11, 26, 72
Cupp, Rod 86, 108
"Curtain Call" 89, 90
Dana Jones Agency 30
Dancer, Mix 53, 54, 55, 63
Densmore Hotel (Kansas City) 7, 9

Denver Post 6
Dignan, James M. 29-30
Discussion of Fashions xiv
Disney, Walt 31
Dix, Dorothy 33
Domestic Science Talk xiv
Don Lee Broadcasting System 29
Dorothy Dix on the Air 58
Downs, Bill 95
Drackett Company 84
Drano 84
Dwarfies Harmonizers 15
Easy Aces 13, 59
Edwards, Eddie 28
Eleanor Taylor Bell Memorial Hospital (Kansas City) 7
Ellis, Charles Edgar 4-6, 7
"Especially For You" 87
Evangelical United Brethren Church (Richland, KS) 100
Fashion and Household Talks xiv
Federal Emergency Relief Administration 41
Ferry-Hanly Advertising Company 18, 26, 36, 37
Fibber McGee & Molly 14, 45
Flanders, Lydia xiv
Flath, P. Hans 20, 23
Food Fads and Fancies xiv
Fox, J. Leslie 27
Frankel, Mortimer 95
"Fun With Facts" 89, 90, 92, 93
Gallup, Alice 92, 93
Gamma Alpha Chi 87
Garden & Home Beautifying xiii
General Mills xv, 45, 47-50, 53-59, 63-64, 66-70, 91, 101
General Mills Hour 55
Gibson, Maxine 50
Gland-O-Lac Co. 84
Gold Medal Kitchen Tested Flour xiii, 47, 48, 57, 65
Good Luck Margarine 84
Goode, Nancy 87
Green Acres 14

Guiding Light, The xv, 59
H. D. Lee Co. 86
Haaren High School (NYC) 85
Halley, Dr. George 17, 64, 65, 66-69
Halley, Mondane Phillips 17-18
Halper, Donna x
Hamilton College (Kentucky) 5
Happy Hollow 16, 17, 18, 20, 22, 28
Happy Hollow Bugle, The 17, 36
Happy Home, The 76-78, 82, 84, 85, 86, 88, 96, 97-99, 103-119
Happy Kitchen, The 41-42, 87-88, 97
Harry, Virginia 20
Harvard University 5
Health Assurance xiv
Heinz 43
Henning, Paul 14
Heyser, Fran 48, 50-55, 58, 63, 64, 66, 76, 97, 116,
Hilmes, Michelle ix
Hints for Housekeeper xiv
Hollanderizin Corporation 84
Home Economics xiv
Home Furnishing - Modern and Practical xiii
homemaking (radio broadcasts) xii-xiv
Home Management xiv
Home Service Talk xiv
Hooper ratings 67, 95
Hooper, C. E. 95
Hoover, Herbert 10
Horner, Charles 21
House By the Side of the Road, The 59
House of Heinz, The 43
Household Hints xiv
Housekeeper's Half Hour xiv
Housewife's Hour, The xiii
Howard, Ora 35
Huckins, Janet 63, 64, 66, 67-69
Hughes, Reavis x
Hummert, Anne xv, 75
Hummert, Frank xv, 75
Hurst, Matilda P. 2
Husted, Marjorie 55

Incredible, But True 43
"Inside the News" 89, 90, 93
Institute for Education by Radio 91
Iowa Barn Dance 59
Iowa State University 87
J. L. Hudson Store 10, 11 26
J. Walter Thompson 43
Jack Armstrong, All American Boy 58, 67
Jardine, Winnifred Cannon (see Cannon, Winnifred)
Jenkins, Dr. Burris 5-6, 8, 26-27, 100
Joanne Taylor's Fashion Flashes 26-35, 36, 37, 38, 45, 70, 86, 87, 97, 101,
Joanne Taylor's Strolling Juvenile Players 31, 32
John J. Jelke Company 84
John Taylor Dry Goods, Co. 26 - 36, 38, 63, 97
Johnny McMaus Midland Theatre 31
Johnson, Bea 33-34, 86-88, 97, 98, 99
Johnson, Rev. Thomas 1
Jones Store, The 26
Jones, Virginia "Ginger" 57, 59
Joyce Jordan, M.D. xv
Junior Artists' Club 22
Kansas Authors Club 9
Kansas City Conservatory of Music 20
Kansas City Electric Association 88
Kansas City Journal 35-36
Kansas City Junior College 94
Kansas City Post 5, 35
Kansas City Power & Light Co. 88
Kansas City Star 10, 12, 25
Kansas Gas & Electric Co. 87
Kansas-Nebraska Act 1
Karr, Elma Eaton 23
Kay Fairchild, Stepmother 59
Kay, Joan 57, 59
KDKA xiii
Kearney, Beulah 41-44, 88
Kellogg 43
Kentucky Wesleyan College 5
KFI xiii

KFOA xiv
KFRM 88, 91, 92, 97
KGO xiv
KGW xiii
KHJ 29-30
Kilmer, Bill 50
Kitty Keene, Inc. 58, 59
KLX xiv
KMA xiii, xiv
KMBC Magazine of the Air 58
KMBC Radio Schoolhouse 89
KMBC, history 12-25
KMBC, performers 13-25
KMBC, women on the station 14-25
Knox Gelatine 43
KOAC xiv
Koerper, Karl 95
Koewing, Jessie E. xi
KPO xiv
Krahl, Kenneth 95
KSAL 86
KTRH 58
KYW xiii, xiv
Lady of the House 22, 23-24, 25
League of American Pen Women 22
Lee, Fred M. 27
Lenore Anthony Theatre Craft School 21
Letters to Soldiers 78
Life on the Red Horse Ranch 38
Lindenwood College (University) 20, 24
Lindenwood College Club 20
Linwood Boulevard Christian Church (Kansas City) 5
"Little Nature Explorer" 19
Little Orphan Annie 58
Lord & Thomas 43
Lorenzo Jones 58
Louise Massey and the Westerners 14
Lowell Press (Kansas City) 22
Lower, Dr. Mary 23
Ma Perkins 58, 67, 77
Mabie, Allen 16
Mabie, Curt "Dott" 16

Mabie, Milton 16
MacBride, Ullman & Ryder 27
MacCormack, Franklin 56, 57, 59
Macy's 27
Maggi Seasoning 43
"Magic Book" 86, 88-94
Malone, Ted 13, 28, 29-30, 36
Marsh Family, The 70, 72-73, 75
Marshall Hatcheries 84
Mary Ann Boy Scout Radio Program, The 19
Massey, Louise Mabie 14, 15, 16
Matney School (Richland, KS) 3
May Company 30
McDonald, J. W. 33
McNutt & McNutt 50
Meal of the Day 43
Mentholatum 84
Menu xiv
Midland Broadcasting Company 12, 36, 37, 45, 48, 50, 54, 63, 64, 66, 68, 70, 88, 96, 98
Midwest Bookman 8
Miller, Hester Burgess 25
Millers' Temp 'Taters 42
Molen, Sam 95
Moler, Ray 95
Montgomery Ward 36-39, 41, 45, 46, 48, 63
Moore, Don 57
Morning, Shari 50
Morrell & Sons 43
Morrow, Marco 9
Morse code ix, x
Morse, Samuel ix,
Mosshart, Crockett 10, 26
Mosshart, George 10
"Music Time" 89, 92, 93, 94
Musical Masseys, The 14, 16
My Lady of the House 25
Nabisco 70
National Barn Dance 16
National Retail Dry Good Association 87

NBC (National Broadcasting Company) 12, 42, 43, 45, 47, 54, 55, 58, 59, 96, 100, 115, 116
Neuman, Kay 88
Norge 43
North-Mehornay Newlyweds 15
O'Brien, Ada Morgan xi
Of Health and Happiness 86
Ohio State University 91, 92
One Girl in a Million 59
One Man's Family 72
One Minute Dramas 95-96
Owen, Dave 55, 63, 64, 67
Packer, Graynella x
Painted Dreams xv
Paley, William S. 12
Parkin, Gladys Kathleen x
Parshall, Josephine Demaree 17
Parshall, Robert 17
Patterson, Ed 7
Payne, Virginia 77
Payton, Keith 92
Penny, Prudence xiii
Peoples Gas Light and Coke Company xiii
Pepper Young's Family xv
Peter Pan Salmon 43
Peterson, Anna J. xiii
Petticoat Junction 14
Phenomenon 58
Phillips, Irna xv, 75
Pillsbury Flour 43
Platt-Forbes Advertising Agency 86
Poehler, Eleanor Nesbitt xi
Poetic Melodies 59
Polytechnic High School (Los Angeles) x
Portia Faces Life 59
Post, Emily 33
Postal Telegraph Company 86
Presbytery of Kansas City, MO 33
Presto Cake Flour 43
Proctor & Gamble 70
Quill Club of Kansas City 5
Quinn, Don 45

Radio Act of 1912 x
Radio Guide 57, 58
Radio Institute for Teachers 94-95
Radio Schoolhouse 88-94
Randall, Eunice x
Recipes xiv
Redpath Bureau (Chautauqua circuit) 21
Reid, J. Lewis 50
Revolutionary War (United States) 1
Rhymaline Time 85, 86
Rich, Jean xiv
Right to Happiness xv
Rise of the Goldbergs, The xv
River to the Sea 70-72, 75
Road of Life xv
Rogers & Smith 58
Rommel, Erwin 80
Roosevelt, Eleanor 82-83
Roosevelt, Franklin D. 82
Rosemary xv
Royal, Ruth 16
Russell, Frank Alden (see Malone, Ted)
Sam 'n' Henry xv
Sargent, Jean xiv
Scattergood "Baines" 59
Schillin Advertising Agency 51
Sears 69, 74, 95-96
Searson, J. W. 9
Seaton, Wretha 19
Sewing Talk xiv
Shawnee Indian Mission 1
Silly Symphonies 31
Skinner, Ted 42
Smith Family, The xv
Smith, Ed 64
Smith, Erle 89, 92
Smith, Gladys 15
Smith, Jack 50
Smith, Woody 15
soap operas xiv-xvi
Songsmiths 15
Spurlock, Nancy 1
St. Joseph News-Press 25

St. Louis Times 25
Standard Oil 51
Stepler, Phyllis (See Kay, Joan)
Stewart, Lee 92
Stickney, James 18, 19
Story of Joan and Kermit, The 59
Story of Mary Marlin, The 59, 77
Studebaker, Hugh 13, 28
Suez Canal 80-82
Sunbrite 43
Sunset Corners 50
Sunsweet Prunes 43
Swift and Company 43
Swinburne, Algernon Charles 71
Table Talk xiv
Talk to Housewives xiv
Talk with Emma Weld xiv
Talk with Sara Prentiss xiv
Taylor, H. Kenneth 27, 28, 29, 31, 32-33, 35, 41
Taylor, Jr., John 37
Texas Rangers, The 13, 16, 38, 75, 76
Those Happy Gilmans 59
Three Arts Studio 21
Three-Flavor Red Heart Dog Food 84
Today's Children xv
Today's Recipes xiv
"Tomorrow's Farmer" 91
Tonight's Dinner xiv
Transylvania University (Kentucky) 5
Travels of Mary Ward, The 35-39, 45, 46, 70, 74, 87, 101
Truesdell, Dorothy 27
United Artists 31
United Nations 77
United State Navy x
University of Indianapolis 5
University of Kansas 94
University of Kansas Medical Center 7
University of Missouri 87
University of Nebraska 9
Unusual Features Syndicate 43
Variety 57, 76, 77, 91, 92, 97

Warner, E. A. 26
Washington Apples 43
Washington, George 1
Waters, Ozie 15
Wayside Theatre 59
WBBM 59
WCCO xiv, 15
WDAF xiv, 12
WEAF xiv
WEBH xiv
Weeky Fashion Letter of Interest to Women xiii
Wellington, Lawrence "Larry" Dilworth 16
Wells, Harlan 10
Westerners, The 16
Westinghouse 43
WFI xiv
WGN xiv
What to Prepare for Tonight's Dinner xiii
WHB 21, 98
When A Girl Marries xv
Whimsies 22
Whiting, Mildred 19, 20
WHO xiii, 47, 53, 54, 55, 67
WHT xiv
WIAE xi
Wide Horizons 70, 72, 74-75
Widmer, Harriet 57, 59
Wiley, Myrtle 88
William Rankin Agency 51
Wilson & Co. 43
Windex 84
Winthrop, Barbara 57, 58
WIP xiv
Wireless Age xi, xii
WJAR xiv
WJZ xiv, 50
WLAG xi
WLS 16
WLW xiv
WMAQ xiv, 55, 57
WMCA 51
WNYC xiv

WOC xiv
Woman in White 59
Woman's Hour xiv
Women's Club xiv
"Women's Daily Dozen" xii
Women's Hour xiv
Women's Program xiv
WOR xi, 50
World Broadcasting Service 38
World War I ix, x, xi, 3, 10,
World War II 10, 13, 35, 80, 82-83,
    87, 102, 116,
WQJ xiv
Writers' War Board 94
WTAG xiv
WWJ xiv
"Youth Looks Ahead" 92, 94
"Youth Views the News" 92
Zercher, Dr. Mary 23
Zimmerman, Marie xi

www.ingramcontent.com/pod-product-compliance
Lightning Source LLC
Chambersburg PA
CBHW051130160426
43195CB00014B/2422